PRIMARY MATHEMATICS 4A

WORKBOOK

Marshall Cavendish
Education

Original edition published under the titles
Primary Mathematics Workbook 4A (Part One) and 4A (Part Two)
© 1982 Curriculum Planning & Development Division
Ministry of Education, Singapore
Published by Times Media Private Limited
This American Edition
© 2003 Times Media Private Limited
© 2003 Marshall Cavendish International (Singapore) Private Limited
© 2014 Marshall Cavendish Education Pte Ltd

Published by Marshall Cavendish Education
Times Centre, 1 New Industrial Road, Singapore 536196
Customer Service Hotline: (65) 6213 9688
US Office Tel: (1-914) 332 8888 | Fax: (1-914) 332 8882
E-mail: cs@mceducation.com
Website: www.mceducation.com

First published 2003
Second impression 2004
Third impression 2005
Reprinted 2005, 2006 (thrice), 2007 (twice), 2008, 2009 (twice), 2010,
          2011 (twice), 2012, 2014, 2015 (twice), 2016, 2017,
          2018 (thrice), 2019, 2020 (twice)

All rights reserved.

No part of this publication may be reproduced, stored in a retrieval system
or transmitted, in any form or by any means, electronic, mechanical,
photocopying, recording or otherwise, without the prior permission
of the copyright owner. Any requests for permission should be
addressed to the Publisher.

Marshall Cavendish is a registered trademark of Times Publishing Limited.

Singapore Math® is a trademark of Singapore Math Inc.® and
Marshall Cavendish Education Pte Ltd.

ISBN 978-981-01-8508-4

Printed in Singapore

ACKNOWLEDGEMENTS

Our special thanks to Richard Askey, Professor of Mathematics (University of Wisconsin, Madison), Yoram Sagher, Professor of Mathematics (University of Illinois, Chicago), and Madge Goldman, President (Gabriella and Paul Rosenbaum Foundation), for their indispensable advice and suggestions in the production of Primary Mathematics (U.S. Edition).

P9-APY-190

CONTENTS

BLANK

EXERCISE 1

1. Write the numbers in figures.

(a)

Ten thousands	Thousands	Hundreds	Tens	Ones
	(1000) (1000) (1000) (1000)		(10) (10) (10) (10) (10)	(1) (1) (1)

The number is _____.

(b)

Ten thousands	Thousands	Hundreds	Tens	Ones
(10000) (10000)	(1000) (1000) (1000)	(100) (100) (100) (100)		(1) (1) (1) (1) (1)

The number is _____.

2. Mr. Wang sold his car for this amount of money.

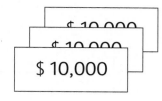 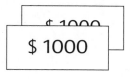 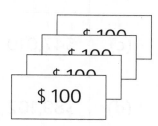

(a) Write the amount of money in figures:

_____

(b) Write the amount of money in words:

_____

3. Write the following in figures.

(a)	Eight thousand, four hundred two dollars	
(b)	Twelve thousand, seven hundred ninety-three dollars	
(c)	Ninety thousand, five hundred eleven dollars	
(d)	Eighty-eight thousand, eight dollars	
(e)	Ninety-nine thousand, nine hundred ninety-nine dollars	

4. Write the following in words.

(a)	$2080	
(b)	$9215	
(c)	$47,010	
(d)	$89,102	
(e)	$40,900	
(f)	$78,999	

EXERCISE 2

1. Complete the number patterns.

    (a) 7000, 8000, _____, 10,000, _____

    (b) 2400, 4400, _____, _____, 10,400

    (c) 4065, 14,065, 24,065, _____, _____

    (d) 5200, 10,200, 15,200, _____, _____

    (e) 9843, 9943, _____, 10,143, _____

2. Write the values of the digits in each of the following numbers.

    (a) 23,529

    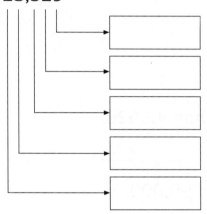

    (b) 40,618

    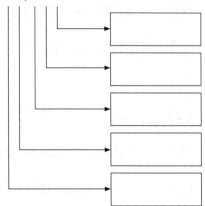

    (c) 45,023

    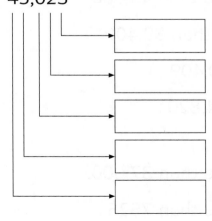

    (d) 88,888

    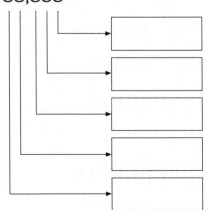

Fill in the blanks.

3. (a) $5623 = 5000 + 600 + 20 +$ _____

    (b) $16,048 = 10,000 +$ _____ $+ 40 + 8$

    (c) $40,180 =$ _____ $+ 100 + 80$

    (d) $72,005 = 70,000 +$ _____ $+ 5$

    (e) $63,100 = 63,000 +$ _____

4. (a) $4000 + 300 + 7 =$ _____

    (b) $50,000 + 6000 + 400 =$ _____

    (c) $30,000 + 700 + 60 + 8 =$ _____

    (d) $10,000 + 1000 + 400 =$ _____

    (e) $90,000 + 90 =$ _____

5. (a) _____ is 1000 more than 42,628.

    (b) 26,324 is 1000 more than _____.

    (c) _____ is 100 less than 90,000.

    (d) 86,000 is 100 less than _____.

    (e) 45,600 is _____ more than 45,500.

    (f) 38,400 is _____ less than 39,400.

    (g) $29,409 +$ _____ $= 30,409$

    (h) $24,830 -$ _____ $= 24,820$

6. (a) 37,526 is _____ more than 37,000.

    (b) 37,526 is _____ more than 7526.

EXERCISE 3

1. Fill in the blanks.

Ten thousands	Thousands	Hundreds	Tens	Ones
7	8	2	4	3

(a) In **78**,243, the digit **7** stands for _____.

(b) In 78,243, the digit _____ is in the **hundreds** place.

The value of the digit is _____.

(c) In 78,243, the **tens** digit is _____ and the **thousands** digit is _____.

2. Fill in the blanks.

(a) In **2**4,568, the digit **4** stands for _____ .

(b) In 43,251, the digit _____ is in the **ten thousands** place.

The value of the digit is _____.

(c) In 30,**5**64, the value of the digit 5 is _____.

3. Arrange the numbers in increasing order.

(a) 3695,   3956,   35,096,   30,965

_____

(b) 43,526,   29,687,   50,314,   46,254

_____

EXERCISE 4

1. Add.

(a)	7000 + 9000 =
(b)	23,000 + 14,000 =
(c)	18,000 + 6000 =
(d)	29,000 + 12,000 =
(e)	46,000 + 24,000 =

2. Subtract.

(a)	13,000 − 4000 =
(b)	46,000 − 12,000 =
(c)	32,000 − 8000 =
(d)	54,000 − 21,000 =
(e)	40,000 − 16,000 =

3. Multiply.

(a)	$3000 \times 2 =$
(b)	$8000 \times 6 =$
(c)	$7000 \times 9 =$
(d)	$14,000 \times 3 =$
(e)	$18,000 \times 5 =$

4. Divide.

(a)	$8000 \div 4 =$
(b)	$72,000 \div 6 =$
(c)	$6000 \div 2 =$
(d)	$15,000 \div 5 =$
(e)	$96,000 \div 8 =$

EXERCISE 5

Fill in the blanks.

1. (a)

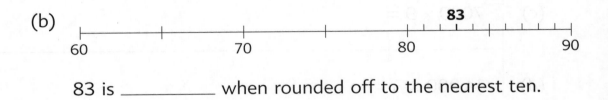

47 is _____ when rounded off to the nearest ten.

(b)

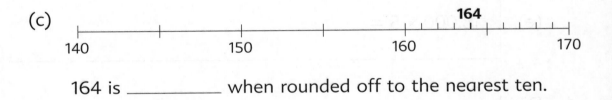

83 is _____ when rounded off to the nearest ten.

(c)

164 is _____ when rounded off to the nearest ten.

(d)

297 is _____ when rounded off to the nearest ten.

(e)

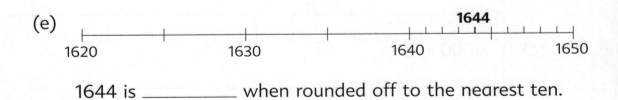

1644 is _____ when rounded off to the nearest ten.

(f)

3447 is _____ when rounded off to the nearest ten.

2. Round off each amount to the nearest $10.

(a)

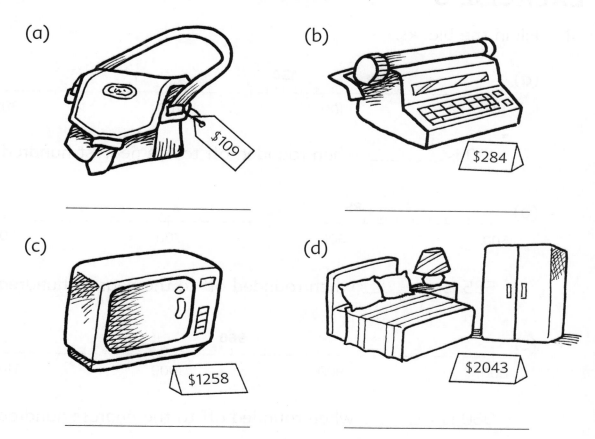

$109

_____

(b)

$284

_____

(c)

$1258

_____

(d)

$2043

_____

3. The table shows the number of computers sold by a company in the first six months of the year.
Round off each number to the nearest ten.

Month	Number of computers	Rounded off to the nearest ten
January	438	
February	272	
March	103	
April	598	
May	346	
June	269	

EXERCISE 6

1. Fill in the blanks.

(a)

130 is _____ when rounded off to the nearest hundred.

(b)

585 is _____ when rounded off to the nearest hundred.

(c)

960 is _____ when rounded off to the nearest hundred.

(d)

1370 is _____ when rounded off to the nearest hundred.

(e)

1860 is _____ when rounded off to the nearest hundred.

(f)

2885 is _____ when rounded off to the nearest hundred.

2. (a)

Ali has 758 books. Round off the number of books to the nearest hundred.	

(b)

There are 3219 pupils in a school. Round off the number of pupils to the nearest hundred.	

(c)

Sally has $2465 in her savings account. Round off this amount to the nearest $100.	

(d)

The distance by air between two cities is 6328 km. Round off this distance to the nearest 100 km.	

3. This table shows the number of stamps collected by 6 boys. Round off each number to the nearest hundred.

Name	Number of stamps	Rounded off to the nearest hundred
Ahmad	705	
Robert	693	
Jincai	1999	
Ravi	5846	
Lionel	1202	
Shunde	2055	

EXERCISE 7

1. Round off each number to the nearest hundred.
Then estimate the value of each of the following:

(a) 319 + 589
↓ ↓
300 + 600 =

(b) 782 − 509
↓ ↓
800 − 500 =

(c) 792 + 204
↓ ↓
[ ] + [ ] =

(d) 903 − 288
↓ ↓
[ ] − [ ] =

(e) 612 + 589
↓ ↓
[ ] + [ ] =

(f) 892 − 328
↓ ↓
[ ] − [ ] =

(g) 1798 + 416
↓ ↓
[ ] + [ ] =

(h) 2304 − 996
↓ ↓
[ ] − [ ] =

2. Round off each number to the nearest hundred.
   Then estimate the value of each of the following:

(a) 296 + 109 + 394
    ↓   ↓   ↓
    300 + 100 + 400 =

(b) 704 − 196 − 312
    ↓   ↓   ↓
    [   ] − [   ] − [   ] =

(c) 998 − 194 + 97
    ↓   ↓   ↓
    [   ] − [   ] + [   ] =

(d) 499 + 301 − 294
    ↓   ↓   ↓
    [   ] + [   ] − [   ] =

(e) 1992 − 607 + 489
    ↓   ↓   ↓
    [   ] − [   ] + [   ] =

(f) 2409 + 593 − 708
    ↓   ↓   ↓
    [   ] + [   ] − [   ] =

(g) 1109 − 98 + 392
    ↓   ↓   ↓
    [   ] − [   ] + [   ] =

(h) 3012 + 996 + 402
    ↓   ↓   ↓
    [   ] + [   ] + [   ] =

EXERCISE 8

1. Write down the factors of 20.

$$1 \times 20 = 20$$

$$2 \times 10 = 20$$

$$4 \times 5 = 20$$

The factors of 20 are _____, _____, _____,

_____, _____ and _____.

2. Fill in the blanks.

(a)

$$2 \times 6 = 12$$

_____ and _____ are factors of 12.

(b)

$$1 \times 8 = 8$$

_____ and _____ are factors of 8.

(c)

$$3 \times 7 = 21$$

_____ and _____ are factors of 21.

3. Find the missing factors.

(a)  $2 \times$ _____ $= 8$	(b)  _____ $\times 6 = 18$
(c) $5 \times$ _____ $= 45$	(d) $6 \times$ _____ $= 48$
(e) $7 \times$ _____ $= 56$	(f) $9 \times$ _____ $= 72$
(g) _____ $\times 4 = 36$	(h) _____ $\times 6 = 54$
(i) _____ $\times 7 = 70$	(j) _____ $\times 8 = 64$

4. Fill in the blanks.

    (a) $8 = 1 \times$ _____

         $8 = 2 \times$ _____

        The factors of 8 are _____, _____, _____

        and _____.

    (b) $15 = 1 \times$ _____

         $15 = 3 \times$ _____

        The factors of 15 are _____, _____, _____

        and _____.

EXERCISE 9

1.

(a) Is 2 a factor of 35?	(b) Is 3 a factor of 45?
$2\overline{)35}$	$3\overline{)45}$

2. Write **Yes** or **No**.

Number	Is 3 a factor of the number?	Is 4 a factor of the number?	Is 5 a factor of the number?
30	Yes	No	Yes
36			
48			
60			
75			
84			

3.

(a) Is 4 a common factor of 36 and 60?

$4 \overline{)36}$ $4 \overline{)60}$

(b) Is 4 a common factor of 48 and 90?

(c) Is 6 a common factor of 30 and 78?

4. Find the factors of each of the following numbers.

(a) 64

$64 = 1 \times 64$ $64 = 4 \times 16$
$64 = 2 \times 32$ $64 = 8 \times 8$

The factors of 64 are

(b) 72

(c) 84

EXERCISE 10

1. Fill in the blanks.

    (a)

    _____ is the first multiple of 6.

    _____ is the second multiple of 6.

    _____ is the third multiple of 6.

    _____ is the fourth multiple of 6.

    (b)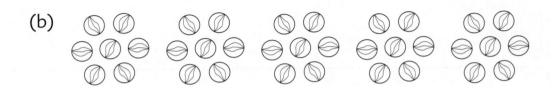

    The first five multiples of 7 are _____, _____,

    _____, _____ and _____.

2. Write the next five multiples for each number.

Number	Multiples
2	2, 4,
3	3, 6,
4	4, 8,
6	6, 12,
8	8, 16,
10	10, 20,

3. Fill in the blanks.

(a)

Multiples of 3:   3, ⑥, 9, ⑫, 15, 18, . . .

Multiples of 2:   2, 4, ⑥, 8, 10, ⑫, . . .

The first two common multiples of 3 and 2 are

_____ and _____.

(b)

Multiples of 8:   8, 16, 24, 32, . . .
Multiples of 4:   4, 8, 12, 16, . . .

The first two common multiples of 8 and 4 are

_____ and _____.

(c)

Multiples of 9: _____

Multiples of 6: _____

The first two common multiples of 9 and 6 are

_____ and _____.

(d)

Multiples of 8: _____

Multiples of 6: _____

The first two common multiples of 8 and 6 are

_____ and _____.

EXERCISE 11

1. Estimate and then multiply.

(a)

$$1893 \times 4$$
$$\downarrow$$
$$2000 \times 4 =$$

$$\begin{array}{r} 1893 \\ \times \quad 4 \\ \hline \end{array}$$

(b)

$$4036 \times 7$$
$$\downarrow$$

$$\boxed{} \times 7 =$$

$$\begin{array}{r} 4036 \\ \times \quad 7 \\ \hline \end{array}$$

(c)

$$5987 \times 8$$
$$\downarrow$$

$$\boxed{} \times 8 =$$

$$\begin{array}{r} 5987 \\ \times \quad 8 \\ \hline \end{array}$$

(d)

$$8195 \times 9$$
$$\downarrow$$

$$\boxed{} \times 9 =$$

$$\begin{array}{r} 8195 \\ \times \quad 9 \\ \hline \end{array}$$

EXERCISE 12

1. Estimate and then divide.

(a)

$2475 \div 5$

$\downarrow$

$2500 \div 5 =$

$5\overline{)2475}$

(b)

$3594 \div 6$

$\downarrow$

$\boxed{} \div 6 =$

$6\overline{)3594}$

(c)

$4214 \div 7$

$\downarrow$

$\boxed{} \div 7 =$

$7\overline{)4214}$

(d)

$6480 \div 9$

$\downarrow$

$\boxed{} \div 9 =$

$9\overline{)6480}$

2. Multiply or divide.

4 0 3 2 × 3	2 3 7 0 × 5	3 2 0 8 × 9	7 2 4 8 × 6
4)5 2 0 8	3)9 2 0 7	8)1 9 3 6	10)2 5 2 0

Color the spaces which contain the answers to the above.
You will help David find his way home.

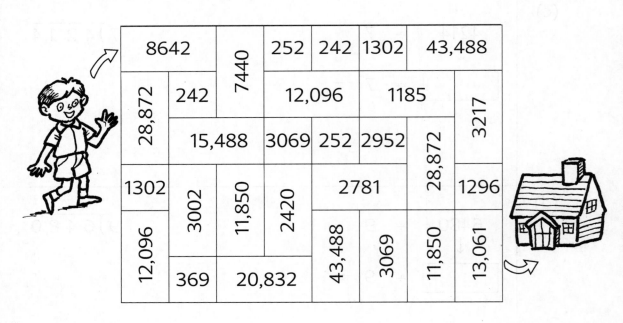

EXERCISE 13

1. A bottle contains red beads and white beads.
   The number of red beads is 3 times the number of white beads.
   If there are 1875 white beads, what is the total number of
   beads in the bottle?

2. The number of meat buns a baker made is 4 times the number
   of curry buns.
   If he made 4864 meat buns, how many more meat buns than
   curry buns did he make?

3. David bought 2 computers at $3569 each.
    He had $2907 left.
    How much money did he have at first?

---

4. 5 people shared a sum of money.
    2 of them received $4356 each.
    The others received $3807 each.
    Find the sum of money.

EXERCISE 14

1. Fill in the blanks.

A car can travel 8 km on 1 liter of gas.		It can travel _____ km on 10 liters of gas.

1 tennis racket costs $34.		10 tennis rackets cost _____.

Justin bakes 586 buns every day.		He bakes _____ buns in 10 days.

2. Multiply.

26 × 10	38 × 10	582 × 10	749 × 10
68 × 3	68 × 30	40 × 5	40 × 50
436 × 4	436 × 40	670 × 8	670 × 80

EXERCISE 15

1. Multiply.

(a)
$4 \times 3 = 12$
$40 \times 3 =$
$4 \times 30 =$

$40 \times 30 =$

$$\begin{array}{r} 40 \\ \times\ 30 \\ \hline \end{array}$$

$400 \times 3 =$
$4 \times 300 =$

$400 \times 30 =$
$40 \times 300 =$

$$\begin{array}{r} 400 \\ \times\ 30 \\ \hline \end{array}$$
$$\begin{array}{r} 300 \\ \times\ 40 \\ \hline \end{array}$$

(b)
$6 \times 5 =$
$60 \times 5 =$
$6 \times 50 =$

$60 \times 50 =$

$$\begin{array}{r} 60 \\ \times\ 50 \\ \hline \end{array}$$

$600 \times 5 =$
$6 \times 500 =$

$600 \times 50 =$
$60 \times 500 =$

$$\begin{array}{r} 600 \\ \times\ 50 \\ \hline \end{array}$$
$$\begin{array}{r} 500 \\ \times\ 60 \\ \hline \end{array}$$

2. Estimate and then multiply.

(a)

$$52 \times 39$$
$$\downarrow \qquad \downarrow$$
$$50 \times 40 =$$

$$\begin{array}{r} 5\ 2 \\ \times\ 3\ 9 \\ \hline \end{array}$$

(b)

$$78 \times 33$$
$$\downarrow \qquad \downarrow$$
$$\boxed{} \times \boxed{} =$$

$$\begin{array}{r} 7\ 8 \\ \times\ 3\ 3 \\ \hline \end{array}$$

(c)

$$29 \times 87$$
$$\downarrow \qquad \downarrow$$
$$\boxed{} \times \boxed{} =$$

$$\begin{array}{r} 2\ 9 \\ \times\ 8\ 7 \\ \hline \end{array}$$

(d)

$$92 \times 71$$
$$\downarrow \qquad \downarrow$$
$$\boxed{} \times \boxed{} =$$

$$\begin{array}{r} 9\ 2 \\ \times\ 7\ 1 \\ \hline \end{array}$$

3. Estimate and then multiply.

(a)

$$218 \quad \times \quad 37$$
$$\downarrow \qquad\qquad \downarrow$$
$$200 \quad \times \quad 40 \quad =$$

$$\begin{array}{r} 2\,1\,8 \\ \times \quad 3\,7 \\ \hline \end{array}$$

(b)

$$483 \quad \times \quad 59$$
$$\downarrow \qquad\qquad \downarrow$$

$$\boxed{} \quad \times \quad \boxed{} \quad =$$

$$\begin{array}{r} 4\,8\,3 \\ \times \quad 5\,9 \\ \hline \end{array}$$

(c)

$$372 \quad \times \quad 64$$
$$\downarrow \qquad\qquad \downarrow$$

$$\boxed{} \quad \times \quad \boxed{} \quad =$$

$$\begin{array}{r} 3\,7\,2 \\ \times \quad 6\,4 \\ \hline \end{array}$$

(d)

$$648 \quad \times \quad 78$$
$$\downarrow \qquad\qquad \downarrow$$

$$\boxed{} \quad \times \quad \boxed{} \quad =$$

$$\begin{array}{r} 6\,4\,8 \\ \times \quad 7\,8 \\ \hline \end{array}$$

EXERCISE 16

1. Multiply and use the answers to complete the cross-number puzzle below.

ACROSS

B	D	F	G
$\begin{array}{r} 21 \\ \times\ 13 \\ \hline \end{array}$	$\begin{array}{r} 17 \\ \times\ 39 \\ \hline \end{array}$	$\begin{array}{r} 37 \\ \times\ 24 \\ \hline \end{array}$	$\begin{array}{r} 82 \\ \times\ 80 \\ \hline \end{array}$

DOWN

A	B	C	E
$\begin{array}{r} 28 \\ \times\ 31 \\ \hline \end{array}$	$\begin{array}{r} 53 \\ \times\ 45 \\ \hline \end{array}$	$\begin{array}{r} 59 \\ \times\ 60 \\ \hline \end{array}$	$\begin{array}{r} 49 \\ \times\ 14 \\ \hline \end{array}$

A		B 2	7	C 3
	D	E		
	F			
		G		

2. Multiply and use the answers to complete the cross-number puzzle.

ACROSS

A	C	D
118 × 23	249 × 31	329 × 18

F	H	J
167 × 17	138 × 11	249 × 25

DOWN

A	B	E
895 × 31	676 × 62	346 × 28

F	G	I
406 × 53	119 × 29	135 × 65

REVIEW 1

Write the answers in the boxes.

1. Write the following in figures.

    (a) Fifty-five thousand, three hundred eighty-two

    (b) Forty thousand, twelve

2. Write the following in words.

    (a) 28,740 _____

    (b) 35,084 _____

3. Write the missing numbers in the following number pattern.

    [_____], 48,615, 58,615, [_____], 78,615

4. What is the missing number in each ■?

    (a) $98,406 = 90,000 + ■ + 400 + 6$

    (b) $10,000 + 500 + 1 = ■$

    (c) $67,014 = ■ + 14$

5. In **47,158**, the value of the digit **7** is [_____].

6. In 69,015, the digit [_____] is in the hundreds place.

7.

Holly's savings

Leigh's savings

Holly saved $ [_____] more than Leigh.

37

8. What number does each letter represent?

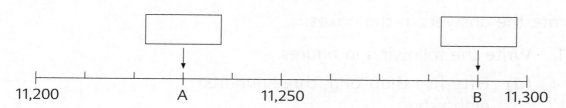

11,200   A   11,250   B   11,300

9. Round off $90,350 to the nearest $100.

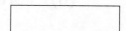

10. Write down two factors of 36.

11. Write down two **common multiples** of 6 and 10.

12. The **product** of two numbers is 216.
One of the numbers is 8.
What is the other number?

13. A shopkeeper had 50 boxes of apples.
There were 24 apples in each box.
If he sold all the apples at 3 for $1, how much money did he receive?

EXERCISE 17

1. Color each figure to show the given fractions. Then add the fractions.

(a)

$\frac{2}{5}$ red

$\frac{1}{5}$ yellow

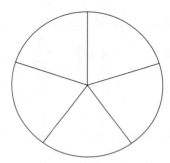

$$\frac{2}{5} + \frac{1}{5} =$$

(b)

$\frac{2}{8}$ blue

$\frac{5}{8}$ green

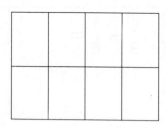

$$\frac{2}{8} + \frac{5}{8} =$$

(c)

$\frac{3}{6}$ red

$\frac{2}{6}$ blue

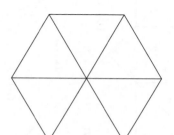

$$\frac{3}{6} + \frac{2}{6} =$$

(d)

$\frac{4}{10}$ yellow

$\frac{3}{10}$ red

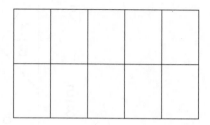

$$\frac{4}{10} + \frac{3}{10} =$$

2. Add. Write the answers in simplest form.

(a) $\dfrac{1}{2} + \dfrac{1}{2} =$	(b) $\dfrac{1}{4} + \dfrac{1}{4} =$	(c) $\dfrac{1}{3} + \dfrac{1}{3} =$
(d) $\dfrac{1}{5} + \dfrac{2}{5} =$	(e) $\dfrac{3}{6} + \dfrac{2}{6} =$	(f) $\dfrac{1}{7} + \dfrac{4}{7} =$
(g) $\dfrac{5}{8} + \dfrac{1}{8} =$	(h) $\dfrac{2}{9} + \dfrac{5}{9} =$	(i) $\dfrac{2}{10} + \dfrac{7}{10} =$

How many legs does a spider have?
Color the spaces which contain the answers to find out.

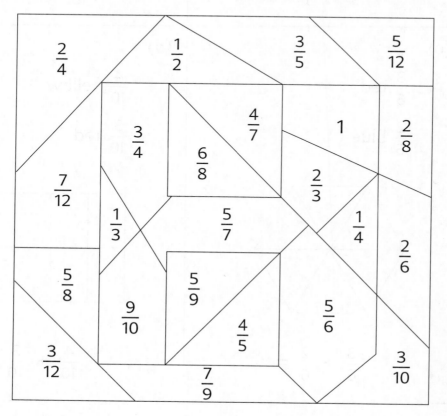

3. Write the missing number in each ◯.

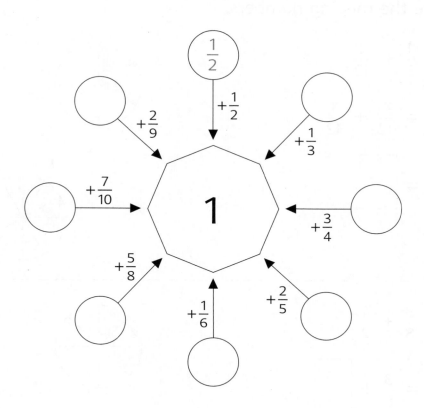

4. Add. Write the answers in simplest form.

(a) $\frac{1}{5} + \frac{1}{5} + \frac{1}{5} =$	(b) $\frac{1}{5} + \frac{3}{5} + \frac{1}{5} =$
(c) $\frac{3}{8} + \frac{1}{8} + \frac{1}{8} =$	(d) $\frac{1}{9} + \frac{2}{9} + \frac{4}{9} =$
(e) $\frac{2}{7} + \frac{2}{7} + \frac{2}{7} =$	(f) $\frac{5}{9} + \frac{2}{9} + \frac{2}{9} =$
(g) $\frac{3}{10} + \frac{2}{10} + \frac{1}{10} =$	(h) $\frac{5}{12} + \frac{1}{12} + \frac{3}{12} =$

EXERCISE 18

1. Write the missing numbers.

(a) $\dfrac{1}{3} + \dfrac{1}{12}$

$= \dfrac{4}{12} + \dfrac{1}{12}$

$= \boxed{}$

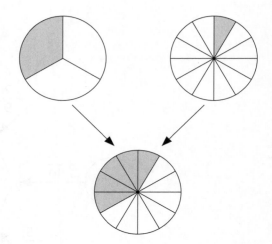

(b) $\dfrac{3}{8} + \dfrac{1}{2}$

$= \dfrac{3}{8} + \boxed{}$

$= \boxed{}$

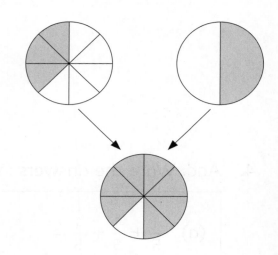

(c) $\dfrac{2}{5} + \dfrac{3}{10}$

$= \boxed{} + \dfrac{3}{10}$

$= \boxed{}$

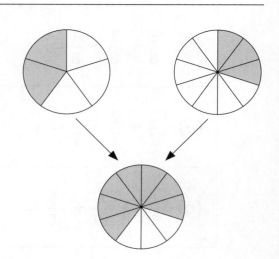

2. Add. Write the answers in simplest form.

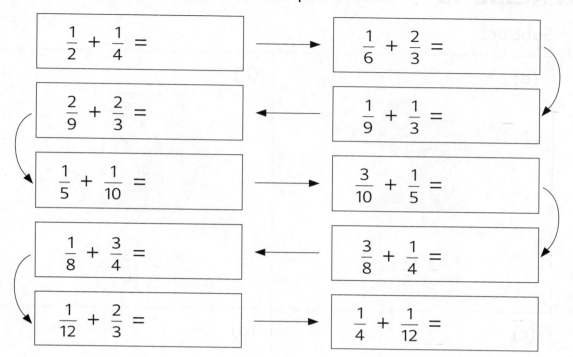

$\dfrac{1}{2} + \dfrac{1}{4} =$ → $\dfrac{1}{6} + \dfrac{2}{3} =$

$\dfrac{2}{9} + \dfrac{2}{3} =$ ← $\dfrac{1}{9} + \dfrac{1}{3} =$

$\dfrac{1}{5} + \dfrac{1}{10} =$ → $\dfrac{3}{10} + \dfrac{1}{5} =$

$\dfrac{1}{8} + \dfrac{3}{4} =$ ← $\dfrac{3}{8} + \dfrac{1}{4} =$

$\dfrac{1}{12} + \dfrac{2}{3} =$ → $\dfrac{1}{4} + \dfrac{1}{12} =$

Join the dots by following the order of the answers above.
You will get a star.

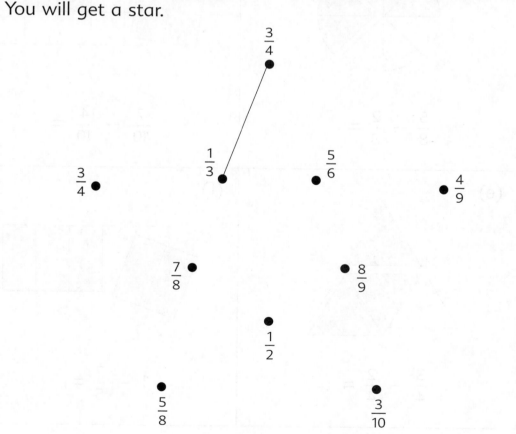

EXERCISE 19

1. Subtract.

(a)

$$\frac{4}{5} - \frac{1}{5} =$$

(b)

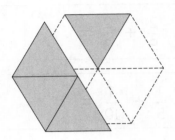

$$\frac{4}{6} - \frac{3}{6} =$$

(c)

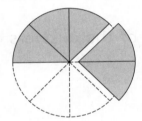

$$\frac{5}{8} - \frac{2}{8} =$$

(d)

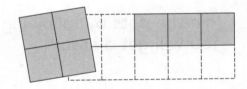

$$\frac{7}{10} - \frac{4}{10} =$$

(e)

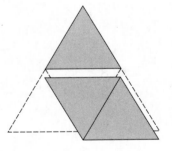

$$\frac{3}{4} - \frac{2}{4} =$$

(f)

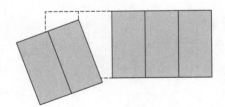

$$1 - \frac{2}{5} =$$

44

2. Subtract. Write the answers in simplest form.

(a) $\dfrac{2}{3} - \dfrac{1}{3} =$	(b) $\dfrac{4}{5} - \dfrac{2}{5} =$
(c) $\dfrac{5}{6} - \dfrac{1}{6} =$	(d) $\dfrac{7}{8} - \dfrac{2}{8} =$
(e) $\dfrac{5}{8} - \dfrac{3}{8} =$	(f) $\dfrac{7}{8} - \dfrac{1}{8} =$
(g) $\dfrac{9}{10} - \dfrac{3}{10} =$	(h) $\dfrac{7}{10} - \dfrac{4}{10} =$
(i) $\dfrac{11}{12} - \dfrac{5}{12} =$	(j) $\dfrac{7}{12} - \dfrac{6}{12} =$

What is two times seven?
Color the spaces which contain the answers to find out.

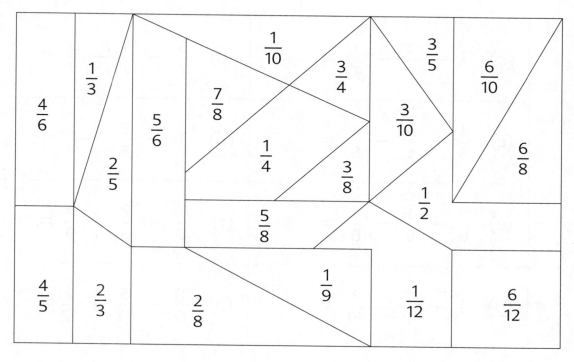

45

3. Write the missing number in each ◯.

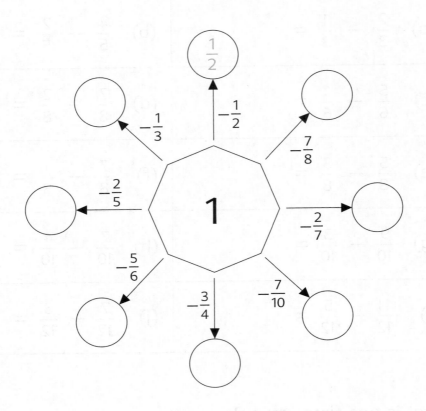

4. Subtract. Write the answers in simplest form.

(a) $1 - \dfrac{1}{4} - \dfrac{1}{4} =$	(b) $\dfrac{5}{7} - \dfrac{1}{7} - \dfrac{2}{7} =$
(c) $\dfrac{4}{5} - \dfrac{3}{5} - \dfrac{1}{5} =$	(d) $1 - \dfrac{3}{8} - \dfrac{5}{8} =$
(e) $\dfrac{5}{6} - \dfrac{1}{6} - \dfrac{1}{6} =$	(f) $\dfrac{7}{9} - \dfrac{2}{9} - \dfrac{2}{9} =$
(g) $1 - \dfrac{1}{10} - \dfrac{3}{10} =$	(h) $\dfrac{11}{12} - \dfrac{5}{12} - \dfrac{2}{12} =$

EXERCISE 20

1. Write the missing numbers.

(a) $\dfrac{3}{4} - \dfrac{1}{2}$

   $= \dfrac{3}{4} - \dfrac{2}{4}$

   $= \boxed{}$

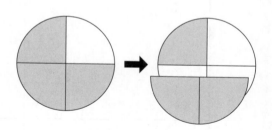

(b) $\dfrac{5}{6} - \dfrac{2}{3}$

   $= \dfrac{5}{6} - \boxed{}$

   $= \boxed{}$

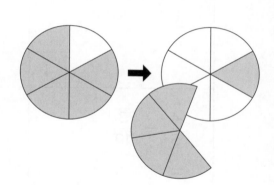

(c) $\dfrac{2}{3} - \dfrac{1}{12}$

   $= \boxed{} - \dfrac{1}{12}$

   $= \boxed{}$

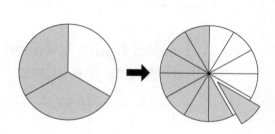

2. Subtract. Write the answers in simplest form.

$\dfrac{1}{2} - \dfrac{1}{6}$ = **A**	$\dfrac{3}{4} - \dfrac{5}{8}$ = **D**	$\dfrac{2}{3} - \dfrac{2}{9}$ = **E**
$\dfrac{3}{4} - \dfrac{1}{12}$ = **I**	$\dfrac{2}{5} - \dfrac{1}{10}$ = **L**	$\dfrac{5}{6} - \dfrac{5}{12}$ = **Q**
$\dfrac{4}{5} - \dfrac{3}{10}$ = **R**	$\dfrac{1}{2} - \dfrac{5}{12}$ = **T**	$\dfrac{7}{12} - \dfrac{1}{3}$ = **U**

A 3-sided figure is called a triangle. What is a 4-sided figure called? Write the letters which match the answers to find out.

$\dfrac{5}{12}$	$\dfrac{1}{4}$	$\dfrac{1}{3}$	$\dfrac{1}{8}$	$\dfrac{1}{2}$	$\dfrac{2}{3}$	$\dfrac{3}{10}$	$\dfrac{1}{3}$	$\dfrac{1}{12}$	$\dfrac{4}{9}$	$\dfrac{1}{2}$	$\dfrac{1}{3}$	$\dfrac{3}{10}$
		A				A					A	

48

EXERCISE 21

1. Meredith bought a piece of cloth.

    She used $\frac{3}{8}$ of it to make a dress.

    What fraction of the cloth did she have left?

2. How much longer is the stick than the string?

    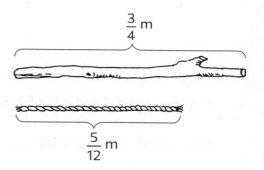

    $\frac{3}{4}$ m

    $\frac{5}{12}$ m

3. John spent $\frac{1}{2}$ of his money on a toy car.

    He spent $\frac{1}{6}$ of his money on a pen.

    What fraction of his money did he spend altogether?

4. Mary drank $\frac{3}{10}$ liter of orange juice.

   Jim drank $\frac{1}{5}$ liter of orange juice less than Mary.

   How much orange juice did they drink altogether?

---

5. Lily bought 1 yd of ribbon.

   She used $\frac{1}{2}$ yd to tie a package and $\frac{3}{10}$ yd to make a bow.

   How much ribbon did she have left?

EXERCISE 22

1. Write a mixed number for each of the following:

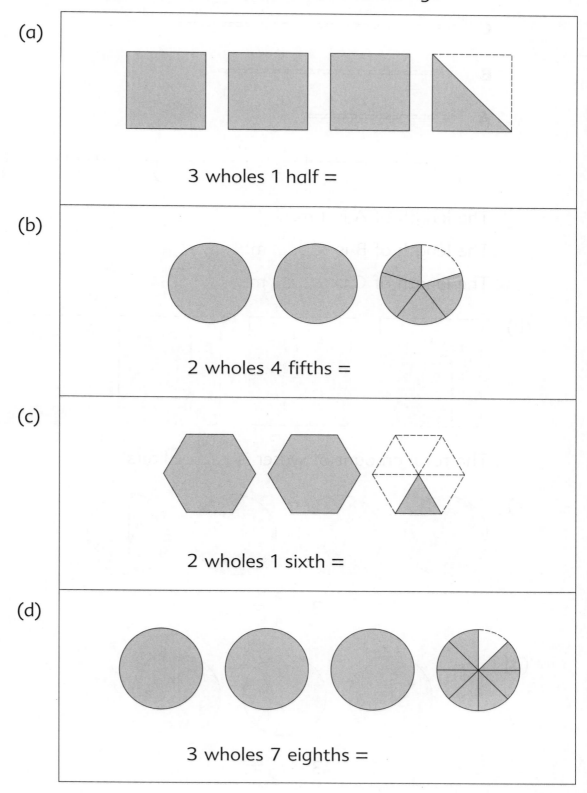

(a)

3 wholes 1 half =

(b)

2 wholes 4 fifths =

(c)

2 wholes 1 sixth =

(d)

3 wholes 7 eighths =

2. Fill in the blanks.

   (a) Here are three strings A, B and C.

   C

   B

   1 m

   A

   The length of A is 1 m.

   The length of B is _____ m.

   The length of C is _____ m.

   (b)

   The total amount of water is _____ liters.

   (c)

   $$3 + \frac{3}{4} =$$

   (d)

   $$3 - \frac{1}{3} =$$

EXERCISE 23

1. Write an improper fraction for each of the following:

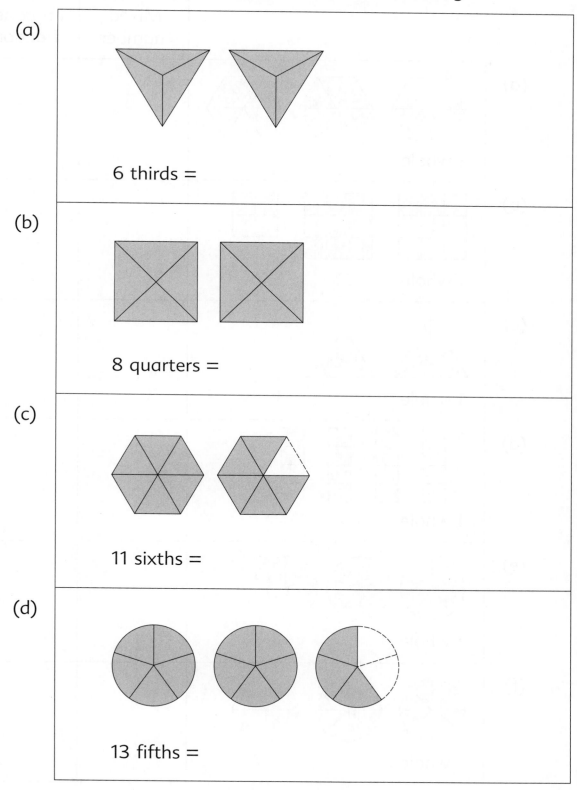

(a)

6 thirds =

(b)

8 quarters =

(c)

11 sixths =

(d)

13 fifths =

2. Write a mixed number and an improper fraction for each of the following:

	Mixed number	Improper fraction
(a) 1 whole	$2\frac{5}{6}$	$\frac{17}{6}$
(b) 1 whole		
(c) 1 whole		
(d) 1 whole		
(e) 1 whole		
(f) 1 whole		

54

EXERCISE 24

1. (a) Express $\frac{11}{4}$ as a mixed number.

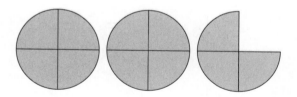

$$\frac{11}{4} = \frac{8}{4} + \frac{3}{4}$$

$$= 2 + \frac{3}{4}$$

$$=$$

(b) Express $\frac{18}{5}$ as a mixed number.

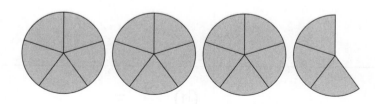

$$\frac{18}{5} = \frac{15}{5} + \frac{3}{5}$$

$$=$$

2. Fill in each box with a mixed number or a whole number.

0   1 $1\frac{1}{3}$ ☐   2   ☐ $2\frac{2}{3}$ ☐ $3\frac{1}{3}$ ☐   4

$\frac{1}{3}$ $\frac{2}{3}$ $\frac{3}{3}$ $\frac{4}{3}$ $\frac{5}{3}$ $\frac{6}{3}$ $\frac{7}{3}$ $\frac{8}{3}$ $\frac{9}{3}$ $\frac{10}{3}$ $\frac{11}{3}$ $\frac{12}{3}$

3. Change each improper fraction to a mixed number or a whole number.

(a) $\dfrac{5}{2} = \dfrac{4}{2} + \dfrac{1}{2}$ $=$	(b) $\dfrac{17}{10} = \dfrac{10}{10} + \dfrac{7}{10}$ $=$
(c) $\dfrac{7}{6} =$	(d) $\dfrac{7}{3} =$
(e) $\dfrac{11}{5} =$	(f) $\dfrac{9}{4} =$
(g) $\dfrac{11}{8} =$	(h) $\dfrac{9}{2} =$
(i) $\dfrac{15}{5} =$	(j) $\dfrac{12}{3} =$

EXERCISE 25

1. (a) Express 2 as an improper fraction.

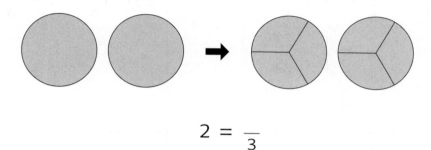

$$2 = \frac{}{3}$$

(b) Express $2\frac{2}{3}$ as an improper fraction.

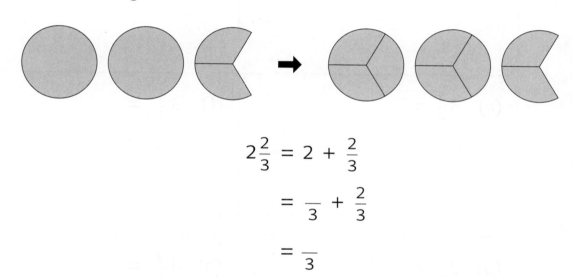

$$2\frac{2}{3} = 2 + \frac{2}{3}$$

$$= \frac{}{3} + \frac{2}{3}$$

$$= \frac{}{3}$$

2. Express each of the following as an improper fraction.

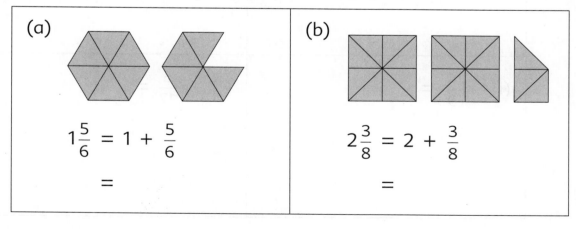

(a)	(b)
$1\frac{5}{6} = 1 + \frac{5}{6}$	$2\frac{3}{8} = 2 + \frac{3}{8}$
$=$	$=$

3. Change each mixed number to an improper fraction.

(a) $1\frac{2}{5} = 1 + \frac{2}{5}$ $= \frac{5}{5} + \frac{2}{5}$ $=$	(b) $1\frac{1}{4} = 1 + \frac{1}{4}$ $=$
(c) $2\frac{3}{8} =$	(d) $2\frac{1}{10} =$
(e) $3\frac{1}{6} =$	(f) $3\frac{1}{3} =$
(g) $2\frac{1}{2} =$	(h) $4\frac{3}{5} =$
(i) $1\frac{4}{9} =$	(j) $2\frac{5}{12} =$

4. Fill in each box with an improper fraction.

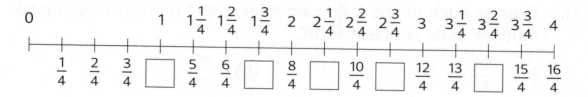

5. Draw a straight line to match each mixed number with an improper fraction.

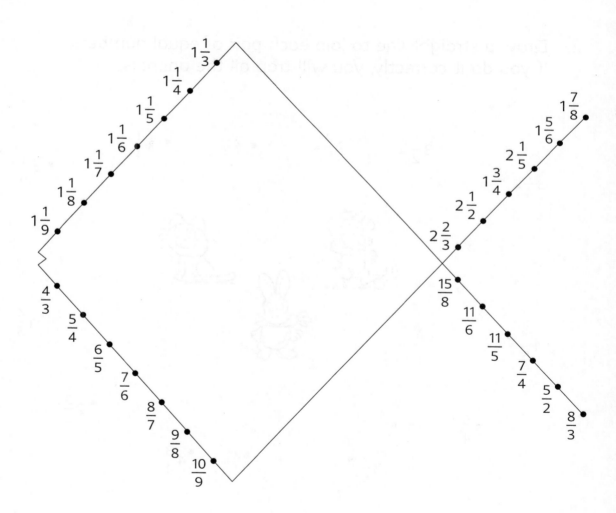

EXERCISE 26

1. Express each of the following as a whole number or a mixed number in its simplest form.

   (a) $\dfrac{12}{4}$

   (b) $\dfrac{25}{10}$

   (c) $\dfrac{15}{5}$

   (d) $\dfrac{32}{12}$

   (e) $\dfrac{19}{3}$

   (f) $\dfrac{20}{6}$

2. Draw a straight line to join each pair of equal numbers. If you do it correctly, you will trap all the animals.

$3\dfrac{1}{2}$ • $2\dfrac{2}{5}$ •   • $2\dfrac{1}{3}$ • $3\dfrac{1}{4}$

$3\dfrac{7}{4}$ •

• $4\dfrac{1}{6}$

$1\dfrac{7}{5}$ •

• $1\dfrac{4}{3}$

$2\dfrac{5}{4}$ •

• $2\dfrac{3}{2}$

$3\dfrac{7}{6}$ •

• $4\dfrac{3}{4}$

3. Add. Give each answer in its simplest form.

(a) $\frac{3}{5} + \frac{2}{5} =$	(b) $\frac{1}{3} + \frac{2}{3} =$
(c) $\frac{3}{4} + \frac{3}{4} =$	(d) $\frac{4}{7} + \frac{5}{7} =$
(e) $\frac{1}{2} + \frac{5}{6} =$	(f) $\frac{3}{4} + \frac{3}{8} =$
(g) $\frac{2}{3} + \frac{3}{6} =$	(h) $\frac{4}{5} + \frac{3}{10} =$

4. Subtract. Give each answer in its simplest form.

(a) $1 - \frac{7}{9} =$	(b) $1 - \frac{5}{12} =$
(c) $2 - \frac{3}{4} =$	(d) $2 - \frac{5}{8} =$
(e) $3 - \frac{4}{7} =$	(f) $1 - \frac{4}{5} =$

5. Write **>** (is greater than), **<** (is less than), or **=** (is equal to) in each ⬚.

(a) $1\frac{1}{2}$ ⬚ $\frac{7}{8}$

(b) $\frac{6}{7}$ ⬚ 1

(c) $\frac{10}{11}$ ⬚ $\frac{11}{3}$

(d) $\frac{10}{3}$ ⬚ $3\frac{1}{3}$

(e) $1\frac{11}{12}$ ⬚ $\frac{6}{3}$

(f) $1\frac{9}{10}$ ⬚ $2\frac{1}{4}$

(g) $1\frac{2}{3}$ ⬚ $\frac{5}{3}$

(h) $\frac{7}{2}$ ⬚ $2\frac{9}{10}$

(i) $\frac{9}{4}$ ⬚ $\frac{8}{9}$

(j) $\frac{12}{5}$ ⬚ $2\frac{2}{5}$

REVIEW 2

Write the answers in the boxes.

1. Write the following in words.

   (a) 60,500 _____

   (b) 42,819 _____

2. Write the following in figures.

   (a) Seventy-five thousand, six hundred twelve ☐

   (b) Eighty thousand, two ☐

3. What is the value of the digit **3** in **63**,029? ☐

4. The digit **6** in **67**,090 stands for 6 × ☐

5. Arrange the numbers in increasing order.
   80,360, 80,036, 83,600, 83,060, 86,300

   ☐

6. Round off 6349 to the nearest hundred. ☐

7. Write down the first 5 multiples of 6.

   ☐

8. Which one of the following is a common factor of 16 and 24?
   3, 4, 6, 48

   ☐

9. Find the product of 23 and 80. ☐

10. Divide 1050 by 5.

11. What is the quotient and remainder when 2490 is divided by 4?

12. Arrange the numbers in increasing order.

$$\frac{3}{4}, \quad \frac{7}{6}, \quad \frac{5}{12}, \quad 1$$

13. What fraction of the figure is shaded?
Give your answer in its simplest form.

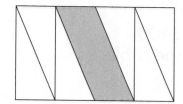

14. The number of people who visited an exhibition was 5350 when rounded off to the nearest ten.
Which one of the following could be the exact number of people who visited the exhibition?

5340, 5344, 5345, 5355

15. Express $1\frac{3}{4}$ as an improper fraction.

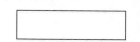

16. Express $\frac{24}{5}$ as a mixed number.

17. Mrs. Smith earns $1750 a month.
How much does she earn in 6 months?

18. Jessica made 1188 cookies.
She packed 6 cookies in 1 bag.
How many bags of cookies did she have?

19. Nicole and Tasha have 2000 stickers altogether.
    If Nicole has 600 more stickers than Tasha, how many stickers
    does Nicole have?

---

20. Jared bought a table and 12 chairs for $2400.
    If each chair cost $165, find the cost of the table.

---

21. 2500 people took part in a cross-country race.
    The number of adults were 4 times the number of children.
    If there were 1200 men, how many women were there?

22. 4 people shared the cost of a hi-fi set and a television equally.
    The television cost $1980.
    The hi-fi set cost $1200 more than the television.
    How much did each person pay?

---

23. A fruit seller had 25 crates of oranges.
    There were 36 oranges in each crate.
    He threw away 28 rotten oranges and sold 786 of the rest.
    How many oranges did he have left?

24. Lindsey bought 12 packets of orange juice.
    Each packet contained 375 ml of orange juice.
    She filled two 2-liter jugs with the orange juice.
    Then she poured the remaining orange juice into a cup.
    How much orange juice was there in the cup?

---

25. Lauren bought 1 lb of flour.

    She used $\frac{2}{5}$ lb of flour to bake a banana cake.

    She used another $\frac{3}{10}$ lb of flour to bake a chocolate cake.

    (a) How much flour did she use altogether?
    (b) How much more flour did she use to bake the banana cake than the chocolate cake?

EXERCISE 27

1. (a) Divide the set into 2 equal parts.

   (b) Divide the set into 3 equal parts.

2. What fraction of each set is shaded?

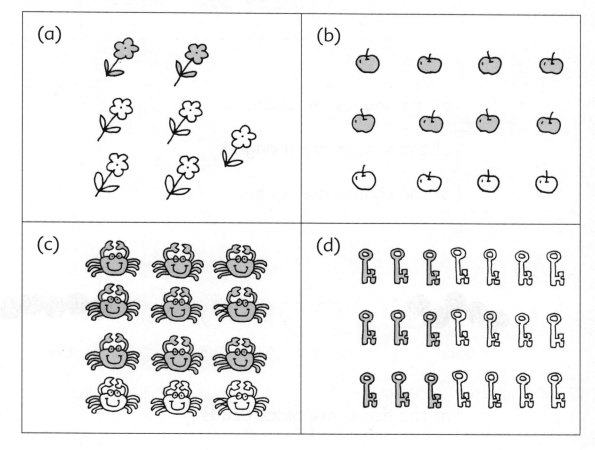

3. Write a fraction in each ☐ .

(a)

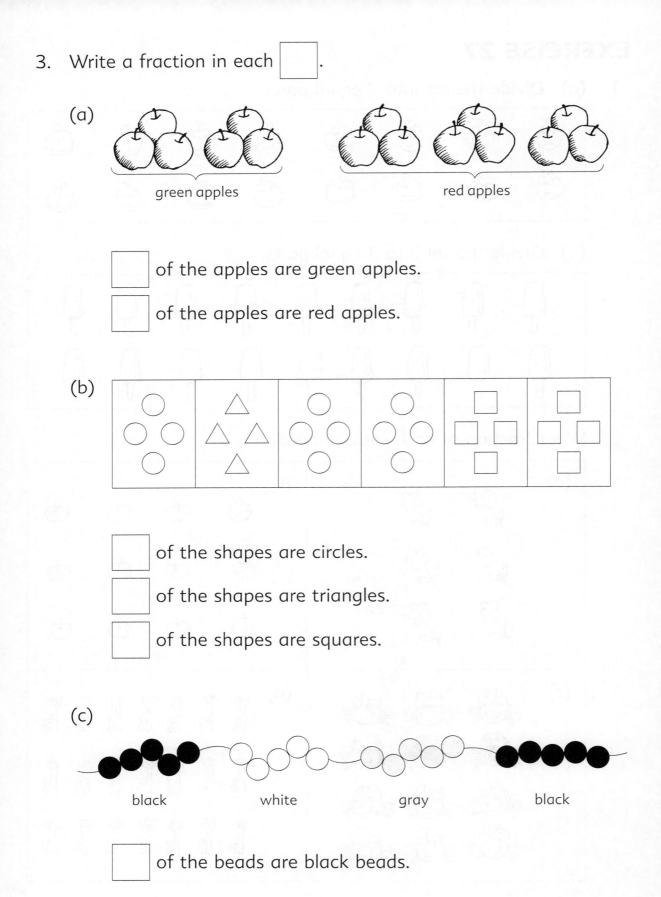

green apples   red apples

☐ of the apples are green apples.

☐ of the apples are red apples.

(b)

☐ of the shapes are circles.

☐ of the shapes are triangles.

☐ of the shapes are squares.

(c)

black   white   gray   black

☐ of the beads are black beads.

68

EXERCISE 28

Find the value of each of the following:

1.

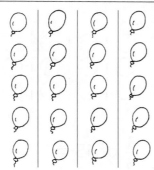

$\frac{1}{4}$ of 20 =

$\frac{3}{4}$ of 20 =

2.

$\frac{1}{5}$ of 25 =

$\frac{3}{5}$ of 25 =

3.

$\frac{1}{3}$ of 21 =

$\frac{2}{3}$ of 21 =

4.

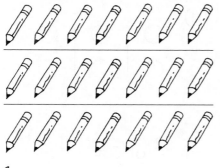

$\frac{1}{10}$ of 30 =

$\frac{7}{10}$ of 30 =

5.

$\frac{1}{8}$ of 16 =

$\frac{3}{8}$ of 16 =

6.

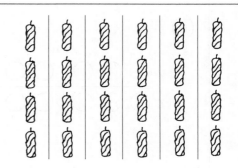

$\frac{1}{6}$ of 24 =

$\frac{5}{6}$ of 24 =

EXERCISE 29

1. Find the value of each of the following:

(a)

$\frac{1}{4}$ of 8 = $\frac{1}{4}$ × 8

=

(b)

$\frac{1}{5}$ of 15 =

(c)

$\frac{1}{3}$ of 12 =

(d)

$\frac{2}{3}$ of 6 =

(e)

$\frac{3}{4}$ of 12 =

(f)

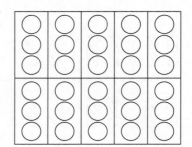

$\frac{3}{10}$ of 30 =

2. Find the value of each of the following:

(a) $\frac{1}{2}$ of $8 = \frac{1}{2} \times 8$

$=$

(b) $\frac{1}{3}$ of $15 =$

(c) $\frac{1}{4}$ of $20 =$

(d) $\frac{1}{6}$ of $18 =$

(e) $\frac{1}{5}$ of $80 =$

(f) $\frac{1}{6}$ of $96 =$

(g) $\frac{1}{8}$ of $120 =$

(h) $\frac{1}{10}$ of $150 =$

3. Find the value of each of the following:

(a) $\frac{2}{3}$ of 15 $= \frac{2}{3} \times 15$ $=$	(b) $\frac{3}{4}$ of 20 $=$
(c) $\frac{4}{5}$ of 30 $=$	(d) $\frac{5}{6}$ of 36 $=$
(e) $\frac{2}{3}$ of 48 $=$	(f) $\frac{3}{4}$ of 60 $=$
(g) $\frac{3}{5}$ of 100 $=$	(h) $\frac{7}{10}$ of 120 $=$

EXERCISE 30

1. Find the value of each of the following:

(a)

 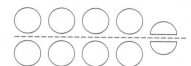

$$\frac{1}{2} \text{ of } 9 = \frac{1}{2} \times 9$$

$$=$$

(b)

 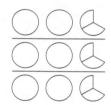

$$\frac{1}{3} \text{ of } 8 =$$

(c)

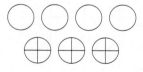 

$$\frac{1}{4} \text{ of } 7 =$$

(d)

$$\frac{3}{4} \text{ of } 5 = \frac{3}{4} \times 5$$
$$=$$

(e)

$$\frac{5}{6} \text{ of } 9 =$$

(f)

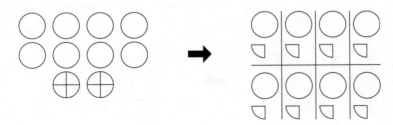

$$\frac{3}{8} \text{ of } 10 =$$

2. Find the value of each of the following:

(a) $\frac{1}{3}$ of 10 =	(b) $\frac{1}{5}$ of 9 =
(c) $\frac{1}{6}$ of 10 =	(d) $\frac{1}{8}$ of 20 =
(e) $\frac{5}{6}$ of 5 =	(f) $\frac{5}{8}$ of 9 =
(g) $\frac{5}{9}$ of 3 =	(h) $\frac{3}{10}$ of 8 =

EXERCISE 31

1. Minghui had 25 picture cards.

    He gave $\frac{2}{5}$ of them to his friends.

    $\frac{2}{5}$ is 2 out of 5 equal parts of a whole.

    25

    (a) How many cards did Minghui give to his friends?

    (b) How many cards did he have left?

2. Siti had $40.

   She spent $\frac{3}{8}$ of the money on a storybook.

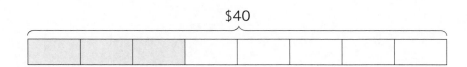

$40

(a) How much did the storybook cost?

(b) How much money did Siti have left?

3. There were 96 people on board a ship.

   $\frac{1}{4}$ of them were females.

   (a) How many females were there?
   (b) How many males were there?

---

4. There are 144 children in the field.

   $\frac{3}{8}$ of them are running.

   (a) How many children are running?
   (b) How many children are **not** running?

EXERCISE 32

Give each answer in its simplest form.

1. (a) Express 20¢ as a fraction of $1.

$$\frac{20}{100} =$$

   (b) Express 80 cm as a fraction of 1 m.

   (c) Express 25 minutes as a fraction of 1 hour.

2. (a) What fraction of 1 day is 8 hours?

   (b) What fraction of one 90-page book is 50 pages?

   (c) What fraction of 1 m is 45 cm?

79

Give each answer in its simplest form.

3. Adam's stride is 75 cm.
   Express 75 cm as a fraction of 1 m.

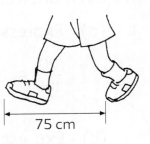

75 cm

4. In a class of 40 children, 16 of them wear glasses.
   What fraction of the children wear glasses?

5. Cameron has 40 toy cars.
   15 of them are battery operated.
   What fraction of the toy cars are battery operated?

6. Jim bought a packet of 60 stamps.
   24 of them were Canadian stamps.
   What fraction of the stamps were Canadian stamps?

EXERCISE 33

1. Limei spent $\frac{7}{10}$ of her money and saved the rest.
    She spent $42.

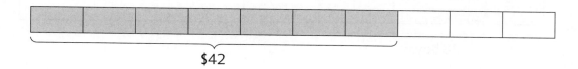

$42

(a) How much money did Limei have at first?

7 units = $42
1 unit = ?
10 units = ?

(b) How much money did she save?

3 units = ?

2. A group of children went for a picnic.

   $\frac{3}{7}$ of them were boys.

   There were 18 boys.

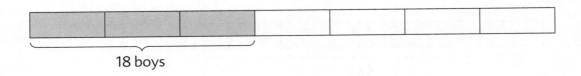

   18 boys

(a) How many children were there?

(b) How many girls were there?

3. Mrs. Reed bought a packet of flour.

   She used $\frac{1}{3}$ of the flour to bake cakes.

   If she used 6 kg of flour, how many kilograms of flour did she buy?

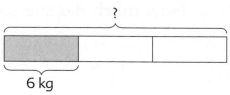

4. Susan spent $\frac{3}{10}$ of her money on a bag.

   If the bag cost $9, how much money did she have at first?

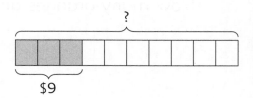

EXERCISE 34

1. Meili had $25.

   She spent $\frac{1}{5}$ of it and saved the rest.

   How much did she save?

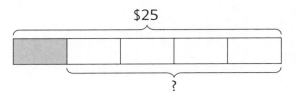

2. Minghua bought 45 oranges.

   He used $\frac{3}{5}$ of them to make orange juice.

   How many oranges did he have left?

3. Meihua had $48.

    She spent $\frac{1}{4}$ of it on a calculator.

    She also bought a book for $14.
    How much money did she spend altogether?

---

4. There are 60 people on a bus.

    $\frac{2}{5}$ of them are children.

    If there are 15 boys, how many girls are there?

EXERCISE 35

1. Travis had 160 mangoes.

    He sold $\frac{3}{4}$ of them at $2 each.
    How much money did he receive?

---

2. Sara bought 30 m of material.

    She used $\frac{3}{5}$ of the material to make 6 curtains of the same size.
    How many meters of material did she use for each curtain?

3. Mary bought a roll of ribbon.

After using $\frac{5}{8}$ of the ribbon to tie some packages, she had 15 ft of the ribbon left.
How many feet of ribbon did she buy?

---

4. John bought some stamps.

He used $\frac{3}{5}$ of them to mail letters.

He had 12 stamps left.
How many stamps did he use?

REVIEW 3

Write the answers in the boxes.

1. 10,000 more than 46,952 is .
   What is the missing number in the 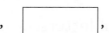?

2. Which is the greatest number?

   85,320,   85,023,   85,203,   85,302

3. What is the greatest 5-digit number that can be formed using all of the digits 7, 0, 1, 6 and 4?

4. Which one of the following is a common factor of 18 and 36?

   4,   6,   12

5. Write down the first five multiples of 8.

   ☐ , ☐ , ☐ , ☐ , ☐

6. Which one of the following is a common multiple of 3 and 5?

   5,   10,   15,   20

7. Mrs. Ricci used 132 cm of lace for her new dress. Round off this length to the nearest 10 cm.

8. What fraction of the figure is shaded?

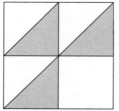

9. Write the number represented by each letter.

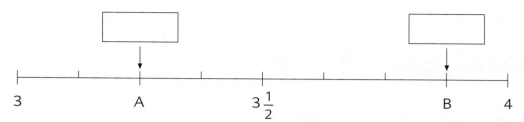

10. A computer costs $1857.
    This is 3 times the cost of a printer.
    How much does the printer cost?

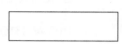

11. If Miguel earns $1460 a month, how much does
    he earn in 6 months?

12. Which one of the following is the smallest fraction?

    $\frac{2}{5}$, $\frac{3}{4}$, $\frac{4}{7}$

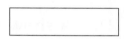

13. Arrange the fractions in order, beginning with the smallest.

    $\frac{9}{7}$, $\frac{2}{9}$, $\frac{2}{7}$, $\frac{2}{3}$

14. Write the missing numbers in the number pattern.

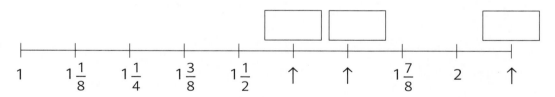

15. What fraction of the fruits are oranges?
    Write the fraction in its simplest form.

16. Express $2\frac{3}{5}$ as an improper fraction.

17. Express $\frac{19}{4}$ as a mixed number.

18. Find the product of $\frac{3}{5}$ and 10.

19. Rosa wants to tie 6 packages.

    She needs $\frac{3}{5}$ yd of ribbon for each package.

    How many yards of ribbon must she buy?

20. Alice made 50 cookies.

    $\frac{3}{5}$ of them were chocolate cookies.

    How many chocolate cookies did Alice make?

21. A show started at 7:15 p.m.

    It lasted $2\frac{1}{2}$ hours.

    At what time did the show end?

22. Brian made 1185 sticks of chicken satay.
    The number of sticks of chicken satay he made is three times
    the number of sticks of beef satay.
    How many sticks of beef satay did he make?

23. A baker sold 35 packets of cookies.
    Each packet contained 150 cookies.
    How many cookies did he sell altogether?

---

24. Devi bought 8 m of ribbon.
    She made 6 bows.

    She used $\frac{5}{8}$ m of ribbon for each bow.

    How much ribbon did she have left?

EXERCISE 36

1. Here are the savings of five children.

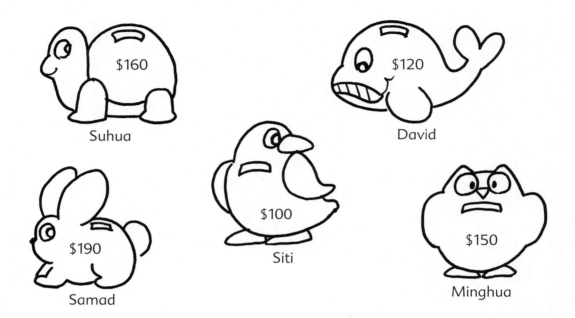

Complete the following graph to show the given data.

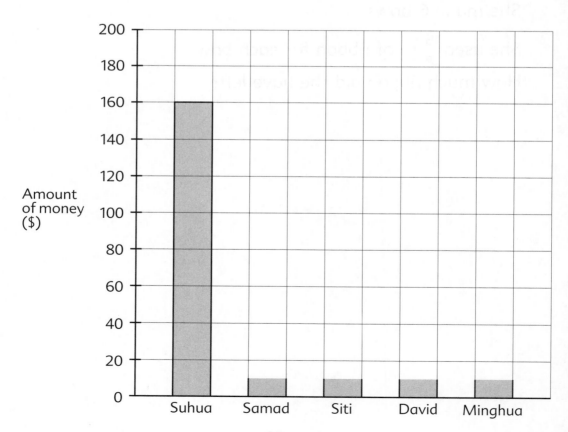

2. This table shows the number of video tapes sold in four shops in a week.

Shop	Number of video tapes sold
A	45
B	95
C	65
D	80

Complete the following graph to show the data given in the table.

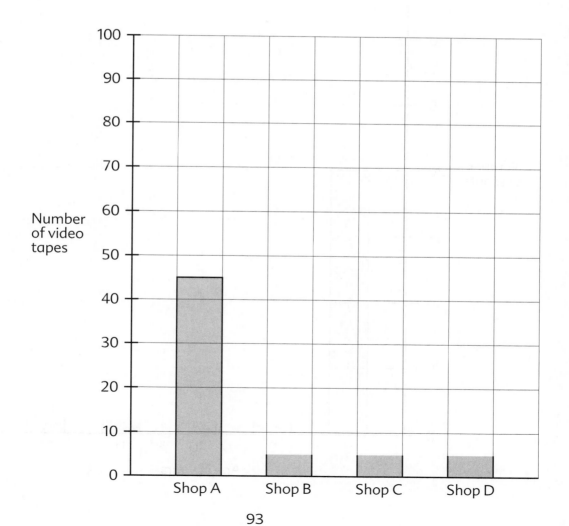

EXERCISE 37

1. This table shows the ages of 100 scouts who went for a hike.

Age in years	8	9	10	11	12
Number of scouts	20	13	18	37	12

Complete the following graph to show the data given in the table.

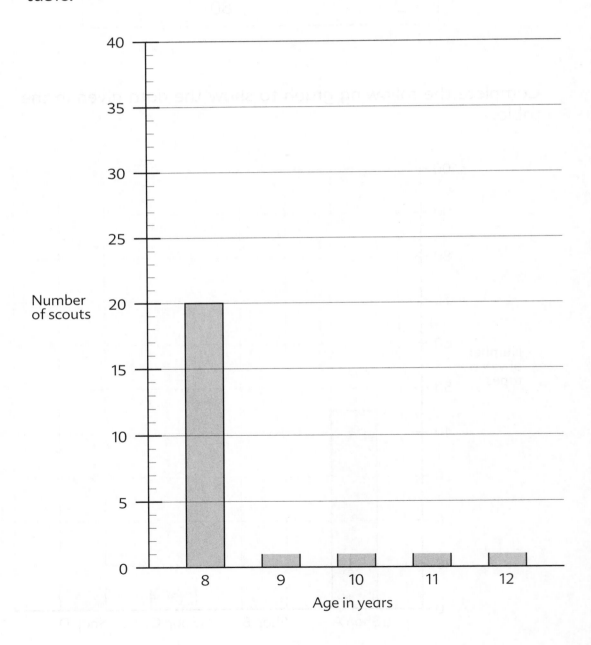

2. This bar graph shows the number of tickets sold at a cinema for five film shows in a day.

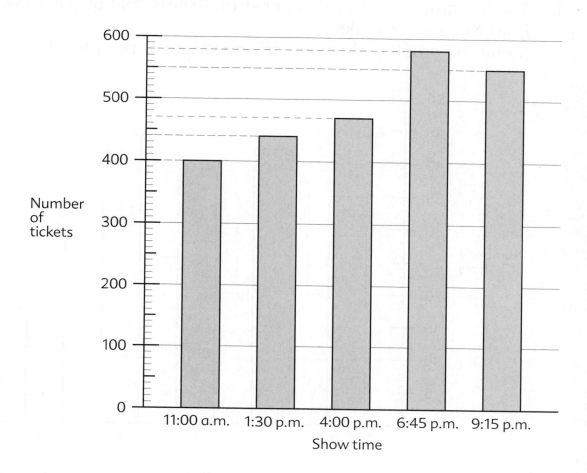

Complete the following table to show the data given in the graph.

Show time	Number of tickets sold
11:00 a.m.	400
1:30 p.m.	
4:00 p.m.	
6:45 p.m.	
9:15 p.m.	

Total number of tickets sold =

EXERCISE 38

1. The bar graph shows the number of T-shirts sold by Mr. Cohen from Monday to Friday.
   Study the graph and answer the questions which follow.

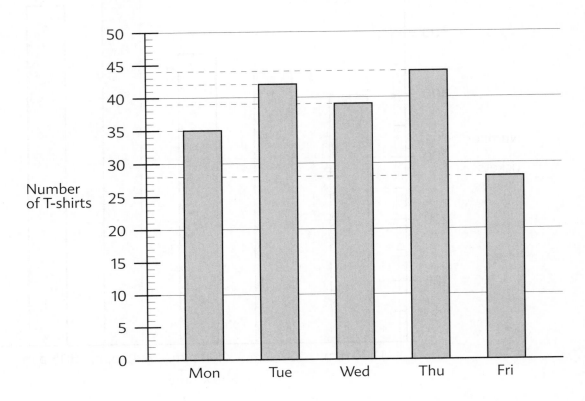

(a) On which day did Mr. Cohen sell the greatest number of T-shirts?

_____

(b) How many T-shirts did he sell on Wednesday?

_____

(c) On which day did he sell 28 T-shirts? _____

(d) How many more T-shirts did he sell on Tuesday than on Monday?

_____

(e) If the T-shirts were sold at $8 each, how much did Mr. Cohen collect from the sale of the T-shirts?

_____

96

2. A group of children were asked which type of stories they liked best.
The results are shown in the bar graph below.
Study the graph and answer the questions which follow.

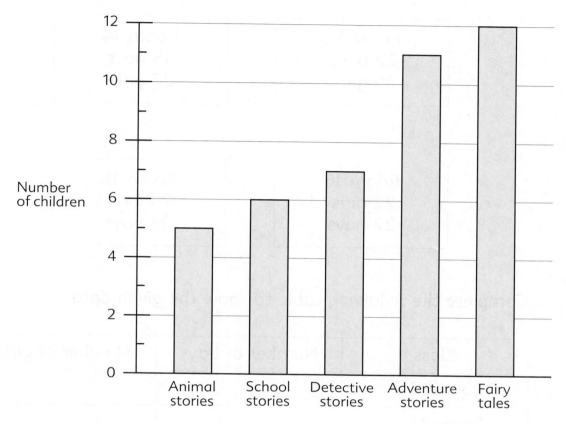

(a) Which type of stories was the most popular?

_____

(b) How many children liked animal stories?

_____

(c) Which type of stories was twice as popular as school stories?

_____

(d) How many more children liked adventure stories than detective stories?

_____

(e) If there were 15 boys in the group, how many girls were there?

_____

EXERCISE 39

1. The number of students in four classes is shown below.

Room 12	Room 14
22 boys	15 boys
19 girls	27 girls

Room 16	Room 18
22 girls	20 girls
22 boys	21 boys

Complete the following table to show the given data.

Class	Number of boys	Number of girls
Room 12		
Room 14		
Room 16		
Room 18		
Total:		

(a) What is the total number of boys? _____

(b) What is the total number of girls? _____

(c) Are there more boys or more girls?
    How many more? _____
    _____

(d) What is the total number of students
    in the four classes? _____

2. The diagram shows the prices of ice cream sold in tubs of different sizes.

small	medium	large
Ice cream 1 ℓ	Ice cream 1 ℓ 500 ml	Ice cream 2 ℓ
$3.90	$5.15	$6.70

Complete the following table to show the given data.

Size of tub	Amount of ice cream	Price
Small		
Medium		
Large		

(a) Mrs. Lee bought 2 small tubs of ice cream.
How much did she spend?

_____

(b) How much cheaper is it to buy 1 large tub of ice cream than to buy 2 small tubs?

_____

(c) Mrs. Gray bought a large tub and two medium-sized tubs of ice cream.
How much did she spend?

_____

3. The diagram shows the prices of detergent sold in bottles of different sizes.

small   medium   large

Detergent 1 ℓ   Detergent 2 ℓ   Detergent 4 ℓ

$1.80 $3.20 $5.95

Complete the following table to show the given data.

Size of bottle	Amount of detergent	Price
Small		
Medium		
Large		

(a) Wendy bought 3 medium-sized bottles of detergent. How much did she spend?

_____

(b) Mr. Dunn bought 2 small bottles of detergent. If he gave the cashier $20, how much change did he receive?

_____

(c) Mary bought 1 large bottle of detergent. Emily bought 2 medium-sized bottles of detergent.

Who spent more on detergent? _____

How much more? _____

EXERCISE 40

1. 5 boys collected some stamps.

   Pablo collected 45 Singapore stamps and 20 U.S. stamps.
   Justin collected 38 Singapore stamps and 15 U.S. stamps.
   Damon collected 65 Singapore stamps and 52 U.S. stamps.
   John collected 50 Singapore stamps and 60 U.S. stamps.
   Jordan collected 22 Singapore stamps and 53 U.S. stamps.

   Complete the following table to show the given data.

Name	Number of stamps	
	Singapore	U.S.
Pablo		
Justin		
Damon		
John		
Jordan		
Total:		

   (a) How many stamps did the five boys collect altogether?

   _____

   (b) How many more Singapore stamps than U.S. stamps did they collect?

   _____

2. The following table shows the number of apple pies and chicken pot pies sold by Marcus in a week.
Each apple pie was sold for $2 and each chicken pot pie was sold for $3.
Complete the table by filling in the total number of apple pies and chicken pot pies sold.

Day	Number of apple pies sold	Number of chicken pot pies sold
Monday	25	34
Tuesday	23	27
Wednesday	24	38
Thursday	30	45
Friday	22	41
Saturday	48	63
Sunday	65	50
Total:		

(a) How many pies did Marcus sell altogether?

_____

(b) On which day did he sell the greatest number of pies?

_____

(c) On which day did he collect the greatest amount of money from the sale of the two types of pies?

_____

(d) How much money did he collect from the sale of the pies for the whole week?

_____

EXERCISE 41

1. What is the size of each angle in degrees?

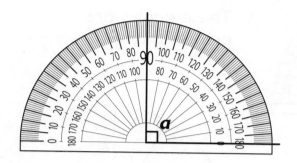

∠*a* is a right angle.
It is 90°.

The following angles are smaller than 90°.

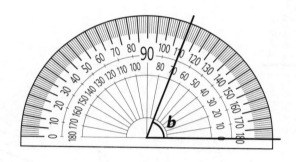

∠*b* =

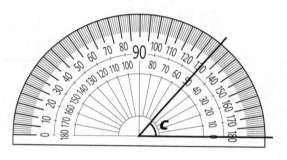

∠*c* =

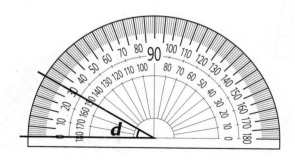

∠*d* =

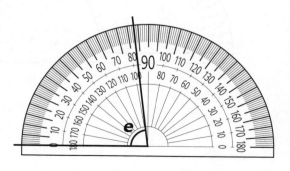

∠*e* =

2. What is the size of each angle in degrees?

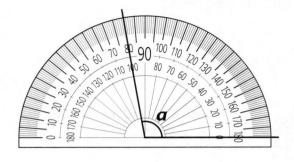

∠a =

These angles are
greater than 90°.

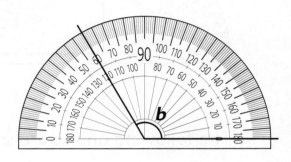

∠b =

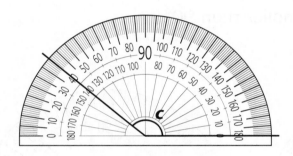

∠c =

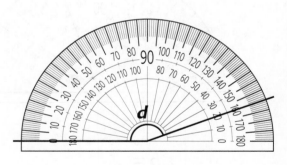

∠d =

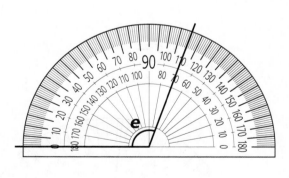

∠e =

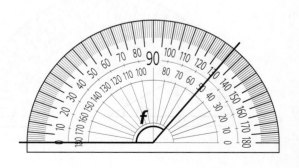

∠f =

EXERCISE 42

1. Measure the marked angles.

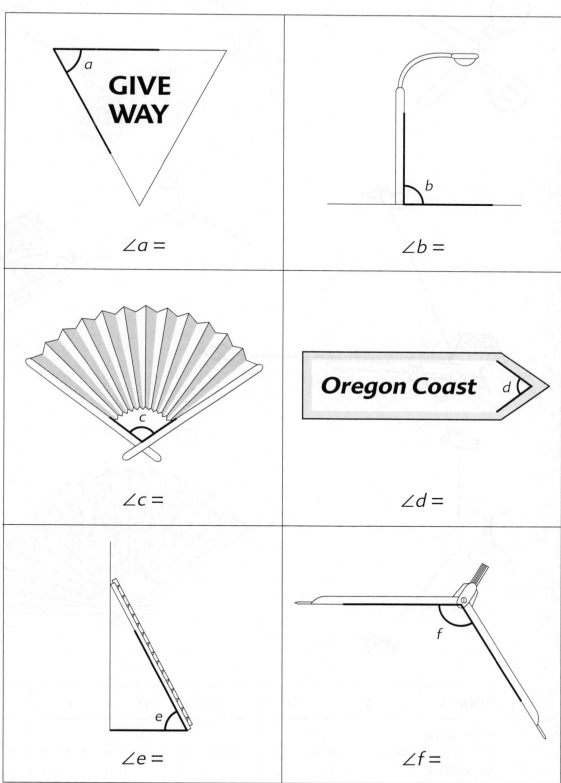

∠a =

∠b =

∠c =

∠d =

∠e =

∠f =

2. Estimate and then measure the marked angles.

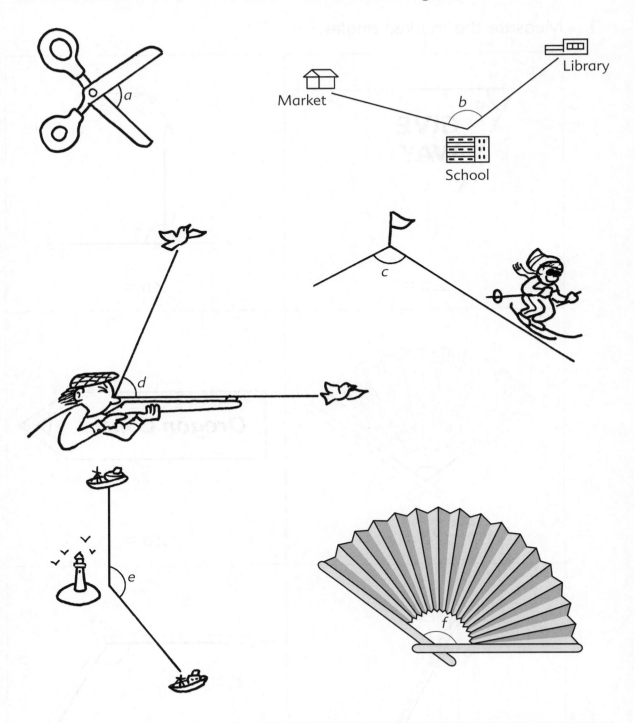

Angles	a	b	c	d	e	f
Estimate						
Measure						

3. Join the marked end point of each line to the correct dot to get the required angle. (Use a protractor to help you choose the correct dot.)
Mark the angle.

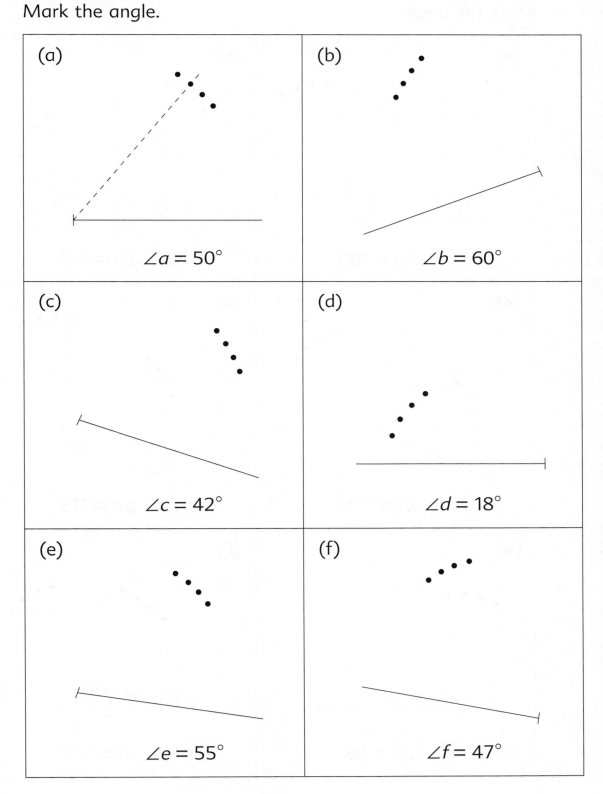

(a)

∠a = 50°

(b)

∠b = 60°

(c)

∠c = 42°

(d)

∠d = 18°

(e)

∠e = 55°

(f)

∠f = 47°

4. Join the marked end point of each line to the correct dot to get the required angle. (Use a protractor to help you choose the correct dot.)
Mark the angle.

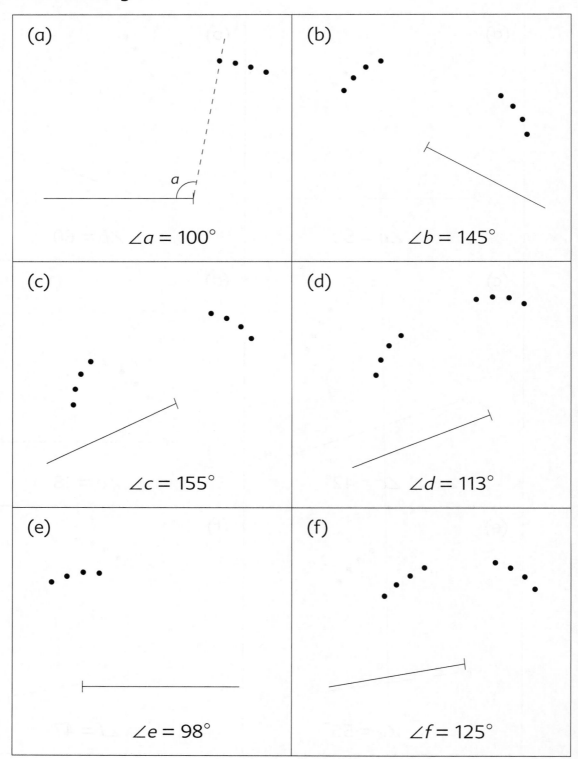

(a)

∠a = 100°

(b)

∠b = 145°

(c)

∠c = 155°

(d)

∠d = 113°

(e)

∠e = 98°

(f)

∠f = 125°

5. Draw an angle equal to 55°.

6. Draw an angle equal to 130°.

EXERCISE 43

1. What is the size of each marked angle?

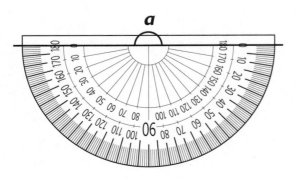

$\angle a$ is 180°.

The following angles are greater than 180°.

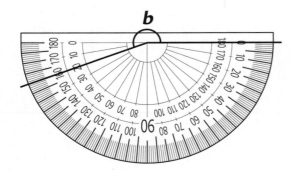

$\angle b = 360° -$

$=$

$\angle c = 360° -$

$=$

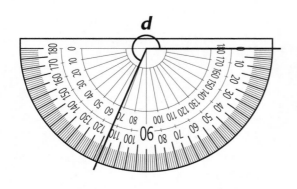

$\angle d = 360° -$

$=$

$\angle e = 360° -$

$=$

2. What is the size of each marked angle?

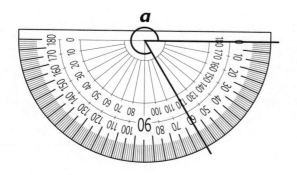

$\angle a = 360° -$

$=$

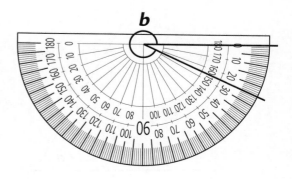

$\angle b = 360° -$

$=$

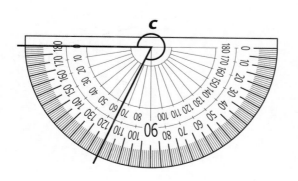

$\angle c = 360° -$

$=$

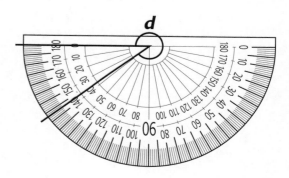

$\angle d = 360° -$

$=$

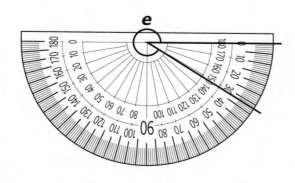

$\angle e = 360° -$

$=$

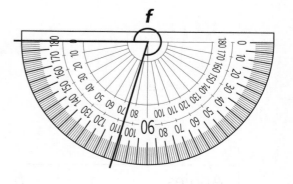

$\angle f = 360° -$

$=$

3. Estimate and then measure the marked angles.

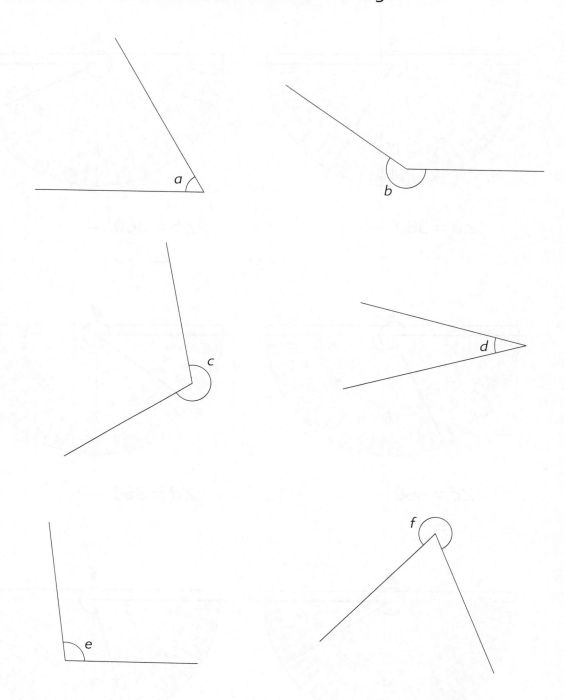

Angles	a	b	c	d	e	f
Estimate						
Measure						

4. Draw an angle equal to 240°.

5. Draw an angle equal to 300°.

EXERCISE 44

1. Find the unknown marked angle in each of the following rectangles.

(a)

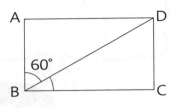

∠CBD =

(b)

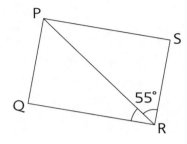

∠PRQ =

(c)

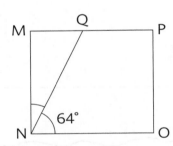

∠MNQ =

(d)

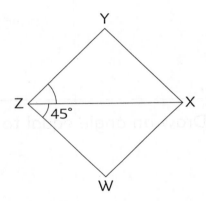

∠XZY =

(e)

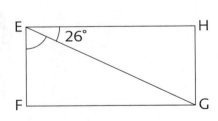

∠FEG =

(f)

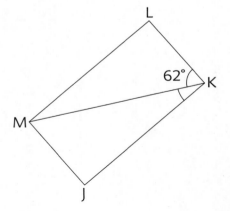

∠JKM =

EXERCISE 45

1. Check (✓) the correct answer for each pair of lines.

	The lines are not perpendicular.	The lines are perpendicular.

2. Name each pair of perpendicular lines.

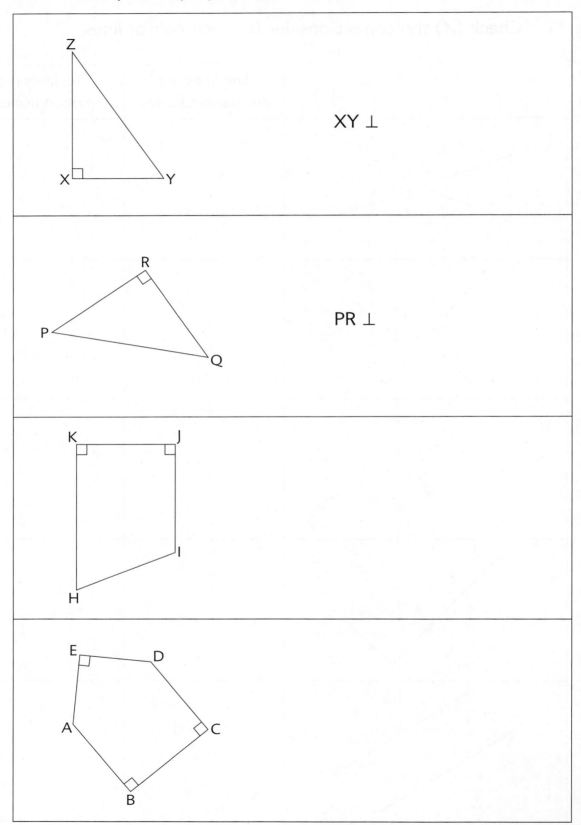

XY ⊥

PR ⊥

EXERCISE 46

1. Using a set-square and a ruler, draw the following:
    (a) A pair of perpendicular lines

    (b) A line perpendicular to the line XY through the point P

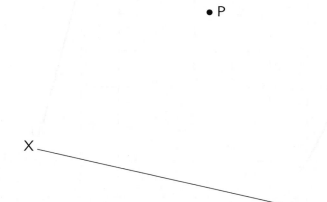

2. Draw a line perpendicular to each of the given lines.

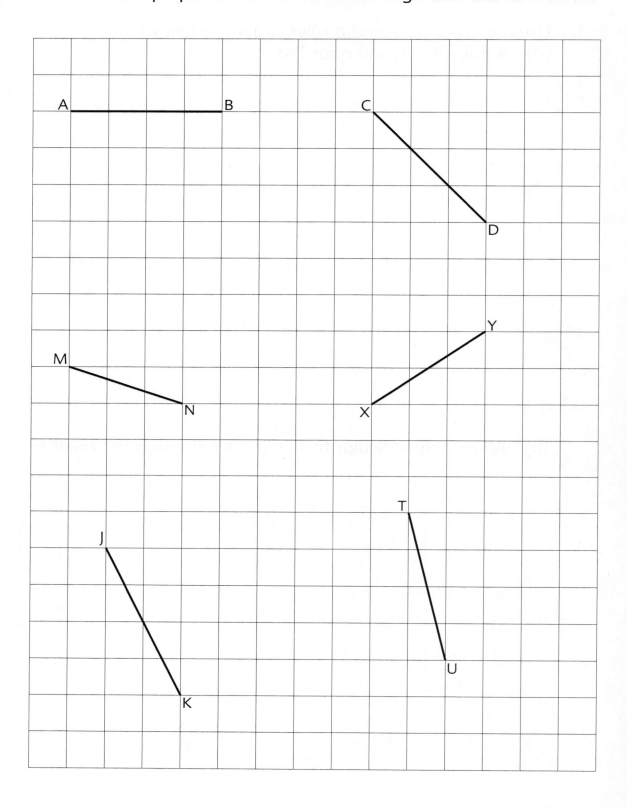

EXERCISE 47

1. Name each pair of parallel lines.

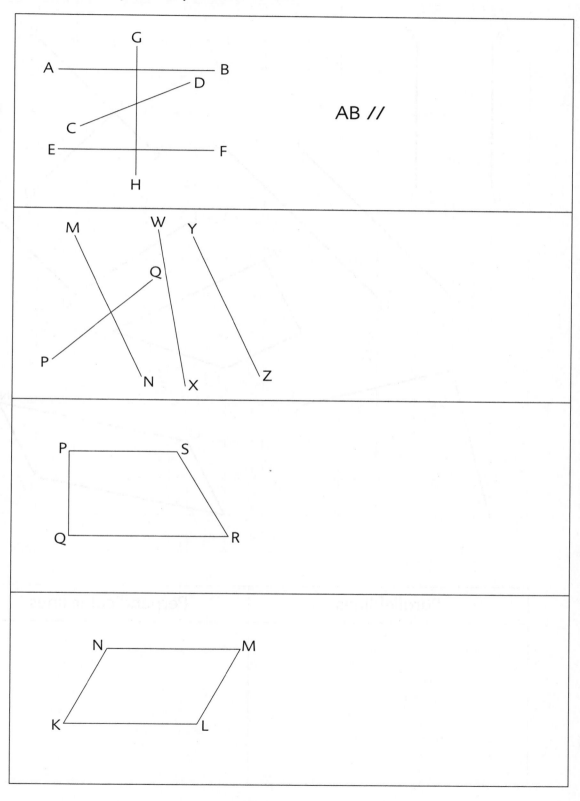

AB //

2. List all the pairs of parallel lines and all the pairs of perpendicular lines in the table below.

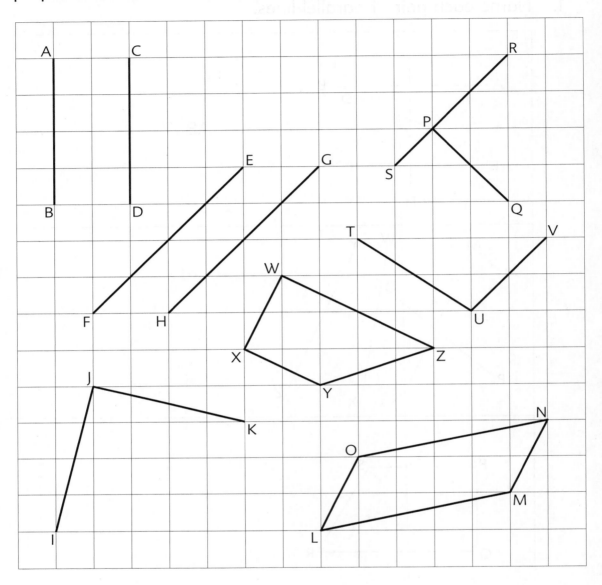

Parallel lines	Perpendicular lines

EXERCISE 48

1. Using a set-square and a ruler, draw the following:
   (a) A pair of parallel lines

   (b) A line parallel to the line AB through the point S

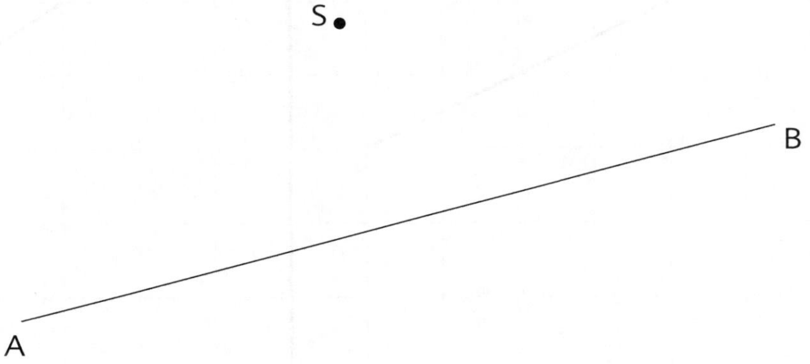

   S.

   B

   A

2. Draw a line parallel to each of the given lines.

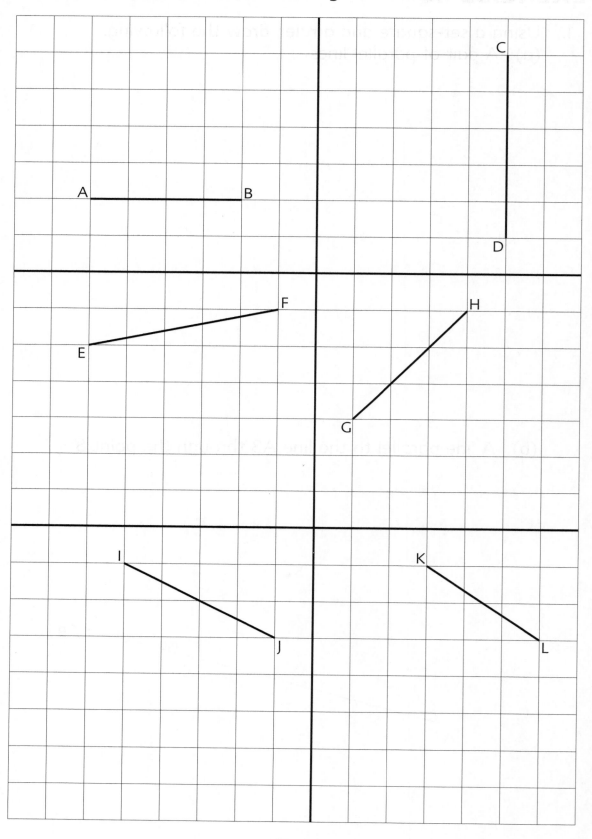

EXERCISE 49

1. Find the unknown side and the area of the following rectangles.

(a)

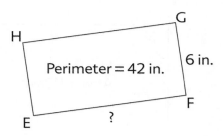

Length + Width = 28 ÷ 2 = 14 cm

CD = 14 − 9 =

Area =

___

(b)

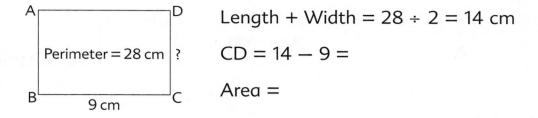

Perimeter = 42 in.

___

(c)

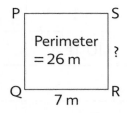

2. Find the unknown side and the perimeter of each of the following rectangles.

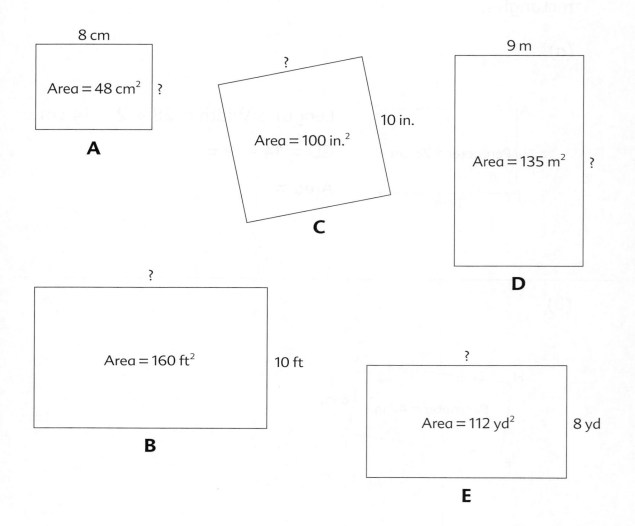

Figure	Area	Length	Width	Perimeter
A	48 cm²	8 cm		
B	160 ft²		10 ft	
C	100 in.²	10 in.		
D	135 m²		9 m	
E	112 yd²		8 yd	

EXERCISE 50

1. Find the perimeter of each of the following figures.
    (All lines meet at right angles.)

(a)

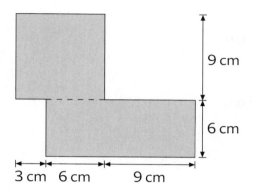

(b)

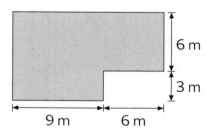

(c)

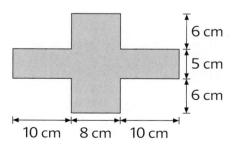

2. Find the perimeter of each of the following figures.
(All lines meet at right angles.)

(a)

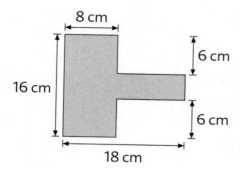

8 cm

6 cm

16 cm

6 cm

18 cm

(b)

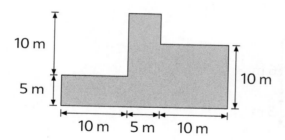

10 m

5 m

10 m

10 m

5 m

10 m

(c)

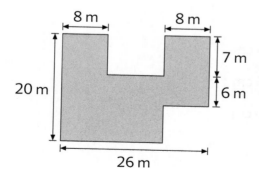

8 m

8 m

7 m

20 m

6 m

26 m

EXERCISE 51

1. Find the area of each of the following figures.
   (All lines meet at right angles.)

(a)

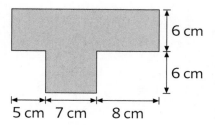

(b)

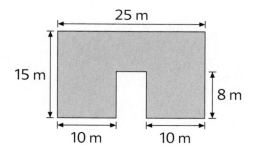

(c)

127

EXERCISE 52

1. Each of the following figures shows a small rectangle in a big rectangle.
   Find the area of the shaded part of each figure.

(a)

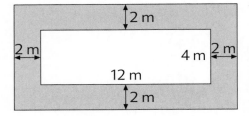

(b)

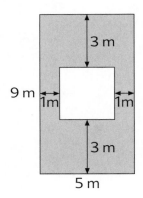

(c)

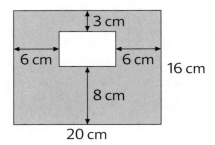

2. A rectangular swimming pool measures 20 m by 12 m.
    A concrete path 1 m wide is paved around it.
    What is the area of the path?

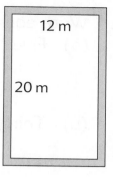

12 m

20 m

3. A rectangular towel measures 96 cm by 60 cm.
    It has a border 3 cm wide around it.
    What is the area of the border?

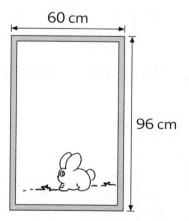

60 cm

96 cm

REVIEW 4

Write the answers in the boxes.

1. Write each of the following in figures.
   (a) Five thousand, seven hundred three dollars

   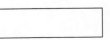

   (b) Thirty-four thousand, eight hundred sixty-four dollars

   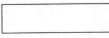

2. When 31,768 is written as 31,800, it is rounded off to the nearest _____ .

3. The digit **3** in 96,3**4**8 stands for 3 × _____ .

4. Which one of the following is equal to $4\frac{3}{5}$?

   $\frac{7}{5}, \quad \frac{12}{5}, \quad \frac{23}{5}, \quad \frac{43}{5}$

5. What is the capacity of Bottle A?

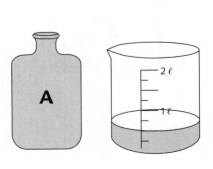

6. Find the perimeter of a square of side 6 cm.

7. The figure is made up of 16 squares each of side 2 cm. Find its area.

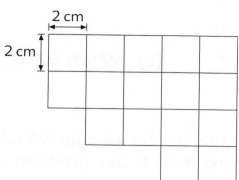

8. The table shows the points scored by 5 students in a test.

Name	Points
Dani	80
Pablo	60
Peter	70
Mary	90
Morgan	40

(a) Who scored 30 points more than Pablo?

(b) Who scored twice as many points as Morgan?

9. In each of the following figures, measure ∠x and ∠y.

(a)

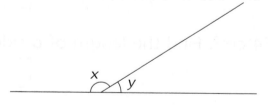

∠x =

∠y =

(b)

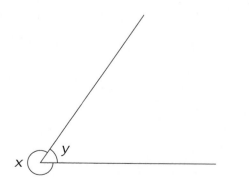

∠x =

∠y =

10.

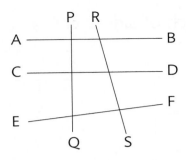

(a) Which line is perpendicular to AB?

(b) Which line is parallel to AB?

11. The graph shows the number of eggs Wendy sold in 5 days. Study the graph and answer the questions which follow.

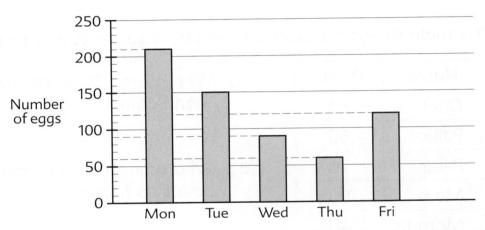

(a) On which day was the smallest number of eggs sold?

(b) How many eggs did she sell altogether?

12. The area of a square is 64 cm². Find the length of a side of the square.

13. Find the perimeter of the figure. (All lines meet at right angles.)

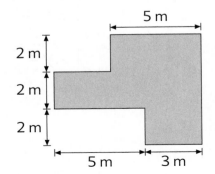

14. A ribbon 1080 in. long is cut into two pieces.
    The length of one piece is two times the length of the other.
    What is the length of the shorter piece?

---

15. Nicky walked round this pond once.
    How many meters did he walk?

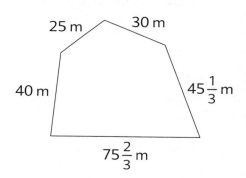

16. A rectangle and a square have the same area.
    If the rectangle measures 9 cm by 4 cm, find the length of each side of the square.

17. A rectangular piece of carpet is placed on the floor of a rectangular room leaving a margin of 1 m around it.
    If the room measures 8 m by 6 m, find the area of the room **not** covered by the carpet.

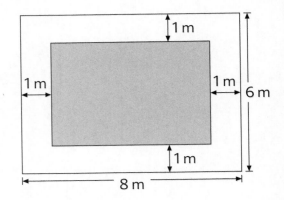

BLANK

BLANK